Feisty

Inspiring girls to think mathematically

Females

Karen Karp

E. Todd Brown

Linda Allen

Candy Allen

HEINEMANN
Portsmouth, NH

Heinemann
A division of Reed Elsevier Inc.
361 Hanover Street
Portsmouth, NH 03801–3912

Offices and agents throughout the world

Library of Congress Cataloging-in-Publication Data
  Feisty females : inspiring girls to think mathematically / Karen Karp
    . . . [et al.].
      p.   cm.
  Includes bibliographical references.
  ISBN 0-325-00009-3
  1. Mathematics—Study and teaching. 2. Literature in mathematics
education.   3. Women in mathematics.   4. Mathematical ability—Sex
differences.   I. Karp, Karen, 1951–
  QA11.F44   1998
  372.7'044—dc21   97-47085
                                                                    CIP

Editor: Victoria Merecki
Production: Vicki Kasabian
Cover design: Joni Doherty *and* Jenny Jensen Greenleaf
Cover illustration: Logan Lake
Manufacturing: Louise Richardson

Printed in the United States of America on acid-free paper

02 01 00 99 98 RRD 1 2 3 4 5

This book is dedicated to the strong women who paved the way for our feistiness through their examples as problem solvers, focused learners, and risk taskers, and to the next generation of young women we expect will take the lead in the years to come:

Our mothers and grandmothers: Frances Harper Laux, June Benson Silliman, Jane Smith Dunlap, Elizabeth Brownley Smith, Barbara Laux Gilliland, Ebba Swanson Benson, and Lillian Rooney

Our role models: Charol Shakeshaft and Eleanor Roosevelt

Our daughters and granddaughters: Beth Brown, Lee Allen, Jessica Ronau, Stephanie Veech, Carin Veech, and Christa Smith

Contents

Foreword

MAUREEN BARBIERI

Girls and math. Math and girls. Somehow the notion of girl mathematicians or mathematical girls seems like an oxymoron. I can recall hours spent memorizing multiplication tables and other math facts in elementary school and then geometry proofs in high school, but I also remember, less nostalgically, the tremendous struggles I had learning algebra and trigonometry. (Calculus was never an option for me, and for that, I was grateful.) In college we hung a poster in the dorm that read, "Have no fear, in real life there is no algebra." Later, taking the GREs caused me horrific anxiety, while balancing my own checkbook was my monthly nemesis. Sadly, my daughter inherited my dislike for math and struggled with it as much as I had. Our experiences are all too common, as girls in schools across the country continue to suffer through math lessons today, feeling as lost and as disconnected and frightened as I did. Such an aversion to math, the authors of *Feisty Females* tell us, can have dire consequences. "Regardless of the personal response," they write, "the reality of mathematics avoidance is that women are often bound by the resulting limitations of their professional qualification and may be barred from careers requiring mathematical knowledge."

Although we shied away from math, my daughter and I loved to read from our earliest days. Picture books, story books, chapter books have always been prominent in our home, and while we read our share of damsel-in-distress stories, books about feisty females are now the ones we seek out and savor, often swapping titles that we find particularly intriguing. If we only had had teachers like Karen Karp, E. Todd Brown, Linda Allen, and Candy Allen when we were in school! We would have read books starring girls and then entered the world of mathematics more assertively, more confidently, more joyfully. Perhaps we would even have found the courage to wrestle with algebra enthusiastically. Perhaps calculating how much room we need in a prospective apartment given the amount of books we own, or making and sticking to a realistic budget, or paying estimates on our income tax wouldn't seem so daunting. Perhaps we would be facing the twenty-first century better prepared for the unknown.

Professor Karp and her colleagues perform what strike me as miracles in class-rooms. Believing that "girls who do not develop inner hardy personalities—who do not become 'feisty females'—may not be prepared to tackle problem-solving situa-tions," they work hard to change the status quo for girls. They introduce wonderful stories to students—girls and boys alike—and then invite them to devise math ques-tions or problems, based on the texts and on the students' lives. And the wonderful thing about the stories is this: They feature strong women and girls, living active lives, behaving in creative and courageous ways, meeting challenges and overcoming obstacles along the way. They are "feisty females," females who embrace the wonder, the logic, the mystery, and yes, the beauty in mathematics.

My husband told me a long time ago, "Words were invented so we could talk about numbers." The writers of *Feisty Females* understand that. The words in the books they read to students lead to exciting explorations into the world of numbers. What they offer students is what Mary Belenky and her colleagues call "connected learning." In these classrooms, girls and boys come to see how integral math is to their lives and to their futures. Girls, especially, learn much more effectively when such connections are made explicit for them, but boys benefit too. It is also impera-tive that boys hear stories about courageous women and understand how vital they are to the world today. The connections the authors of *Feisty Females* make through-out this book are creative and compelling. The students they describe are actually excited about designing and solving math problems, embracing risk, and taking re-sponsibility for their own learning. This is inquiry in its finest sense.

The decision to choose books that present females in such strong light is a wise one indeed. "Girls have trouble with math because math requires what many ado-lescent girls lack—confidence, trust in one's own judgment, and the ability to toler-ate frustration without becoming overwhelmed," writes Mary Pipher. "Girls need to be encouraged to persevere in the face of difficulty, to calm down and believe in themselves."

These teacher researchers have gone beyond new methodologies in the math classroom. Their curriculum is clearly, "hearts-on," as they describe it, and reflects their commitment to honor multiple intelligences and a wide range of learning styles. The children learn by reading, by doing, by talking and writing about what they do, and by reflecting frequently on how it all connects to real life. Readers will find a treasure trove here—an exhaustive list of wonderful books starring compli-cated, brave, gutsy women and girls—as well as many inspiring ideas for presenting these books to students as a prelude to moving into math explorations. But these teacher researchers have gone even further. Realizing that such an innovative cur-riculum would need an innovative system of evaluation, they moved into new terri-tory here as well. The performance assessments and narrative reporting they describe in *Rethinking Report Cards* is clearly more meaningful and more relevant for students than other methods currently used in most of our schools.

Again and again the authors convince us of how essential it is that students come to know and love math as a life skill; the goal is the development of positive attitudes about math in all students. As John Van de Walle put it, "Good mathematics is not how many answers you know, but how you behave when you do not know." I suspect that the students leaving these teachers' classrooms will behave creatively, confidently, and cleverly. They will be unafraid of technology's inevitable challenges and see them as opportunities for positive change, change they can shape.

Helping girls believe in themselves is clearly something these teachers value highly. The classroom conversations, the student work, and the comprehensive list of children's literature all contribute to building confidence, curiosity, and competence in girls. The students that fill these pages are strong thinkers and joyful learners. They will be ready to estimate, measure, calculate, and problem solve in myriad ways, as yet unknown to their teachers. The boys, obviously, will reap the rewards of this dynamic approach to teaching and thinking. But it is the girls' learning I appreciate most. Karen Karp and her research partners, these amazingly feisty teachers, are truly on a mission. They are determined that their girl students be ready to embrace any opportunity, rise to any challenge, and overcome any obstacle in their lives. These women know that, in this complicated, fast-paced, constantly changing world we live in, if you are a female, you had better be feisty. Through their work, they are helping women of tomorrow get a real head start.

Acknowledgments

We would like to offer thanks to the following people for their support and encouragment during the writing of *Feisty Females: Inspiring Girls to Think Mathematically*.

We begin by thanking the Heinemann family for their direct influence on the book in countless ways from the beginning to the published product. First and foremost, Vicki Kasabian, production editor, for her tireless dedication to making a carefully polished product and her keen sense of humor. Also, Victoria Merecki, for her gentle shepherding and energetic marketing of the book. We also wish to thank Leigh Peake for her extensive knowledge of the field of education and her vision in conceiving the initial project.

We thank the female researchers and authors of children's books who we celebrate by incorporating their work frequently throughout *Feisty Females*. We honor their incredible contribution by using their full names in the references so readers can recognize and appreciate the gift women give to others through their words.

We thank the ever-growing community of women and supporters of girls who have shown interest and enthusiasm as we talk about this project at conferences and local presentations.

Fortunately, we all work in environments that celebrate our success and support our burgeoning ideas. To that regard we thank Dean Raphael Nystrand, Associate Dean Beth Stroble, and the Chair of Early and Middle Childhood Education, Diane Kyle, at the University of Louisville. We also thank Charlene Bush, a principal with vision and the gift of empowering teachers to become change agents.

Thanks, too, to our friends and colleagues whose assistance was critical: Deborah Tapp, who experimented with our ideas in her classroom so we could test them in other settings and with students of various ages; Jo Sanders, whose NSF Teacher Education Equity Project provided a catalyst for the initial idea; Maureen Barbieri, who took time from her own pressing deadlines to provide salient insights and heartening words of support; Kelly Thaler, for her attention to references and meticulous wordsmithing; and Dale Billingsley, who gave generously of his precious time to read each word and provide thoughtful editing and invaluable feedback.

We owe a great debt to our female and males students who willingly tried new ways of looking at books, took risks in their problem solving, thought and talked about mathematics differently, and shared their wisdom with us. In addition we thank the parents of the students in the classrooms in which we worked who remained excited about and committed to the special mathematics activities that their children brought home (which in many cases were vastly different from what they expected).

We all thank our families for the time, space, and emotional energy to make this book a reality. We thank Ron, Andy, and Beth Brown; Bob Ronau, Matthew, and Jeffrey Karp; Larry, Ryan, Kyle, Kevin, and Lee Allen. We also remember the support and cherish the memory of David Allen for his lifetime of encouraging all learners to pursue educational endeavors.

To all we say thanks.

Introduction

Framing the Landscape

What literature do you remember reading as part of a required reading list when you were in school? Books such as *Johnny Tremain*, *Ivanhoe*, *Silas Marner*, and *Great Expectations*? Were *Romeo and Juliet*, *Pride and Prejudice*, *The Scarlet Letter*, and *Jane Eyre* the only books whose central protagonist was female?

When the world is described over and over in terms that do not include girls, the message is clear. If girls cannot envision themselves as characters who face uncertainty, seek change with a positive attitude, and take risks with confidence, how can we be sure that they will learn to carry out the roles we expect of them? How can they be continuously asked to examine and investigate the lives of men, how can they consistently be asked to see women in subordinate roles, desperately seeking marriage, or killing themselves over a romantic relationship, and then be told to think of themselves as problem solvers and leaders?

When we look at the discipline of mathematics we find that very few of the graduates in advanced engineering and mathematics programs are women. You might ask how these two schooling experiences, the reading of novels and career choices, are connected. What threads could be used to stitch together formal literary experiences and the avoidance of mathematics-related occupations?

When we do not develop images of women as capable and logical thinkers but as damsels in distress, is it any wonder that although females are taking more mathematics classes than ever before, they still strategically avoid careers in math-related fields?

The well-known British author, Margaret Drabble, reflects on her own recollections of mathematics instruction:

> I dropped mathematics at 12, through some freak in the syllabus. I cannot deny that I dropped math with a sigh of relief, for I had always loathed it, always felt uncomprehending even while getting tolerable marks, didn't like subjects I wasn't good at, and had no notion of this subject's appeal or significance.

The reason, I imagine, was that, like most girls I had been badly taught from the beginning: I am not really as innumerate as I pretend, and suspect there is little wrong with the basic equipment but I shall never know. . . .

And that effectively, though I did not appreciate it at the time, closed most careers and half of culture to me forever. (1975, 16)

After reading Drabble's story, we could not help remembering stories about our own mathematical experiences. We each could recall ways in which gender influenced our mathematics education. Todd's memories mirror an educational history we all could relate to:

I can remember almost the exact time in my schooling when mathematics became my least favorite subject. I was a fourth grader in a small elementary school in rural Minnesota. My teacher was a taskmaster and was famous for testing our knowledge of the multiplication facts in what were known as lightning rounds. These were rapid-fire flash card events where two students were pitted against each other in a race for the fastest reply. As my turns would come, and I made more than one error, the teacher sent me to the chalkboard to write the multiplication tables. To this day I can feel the eyes of my classmates like lasers on my back, and hear the sound of snickers and giggles when I made mistakes. That experience was vivid and humiliating. As a result, I was left with limited self-confidence and a mindset that I could not be good at mathematics. At that moment I began on a long road of unsuccessful mathematics experiences. Since at that time math was only taught by telling, I accepted mathematics as a language I could not begin to understand. Geometry was one of the few math classes that made sense as I could actually see the relationships between the figures and the formulas. I never found my inner voice so that I could shout out and ask for more teacher support, yet through silent communications I became convinced that I could never be good at this subject. I never sensed nor was given any warning that mathematics was so critical for my future. The unspoken message was just to get by.

I continued this struggle all through high school, and was relieved that I only had to take a limited amount of college mathematics to become a teacher. How did that affect me? I have often wondered what other careers I would have pursued if I had had the confidence to tackle more challenging mathematics, or if I had strong encouragement or mentoring from teachers. Most people would have taken this life experience and accepted their mathematical limitations. But my stubborn side gave me the determination not to let this happen to anyone in my mathematics classes. When I first began teaching, mathematics was still taught from textbooks using a memorized collection of abstract rules and formulas. Even then I was sensitive to that look in children's eyes that the mathematics concepts just did not make sense. I knew that I had to find another way to teach mathematics and since I had always succeeded with visuals, I began with base-ten blocks, beans, egg cartons, dice, and other recycled materials I could gather. Initially when I introduced concepts, I was compelled to find ways to integrate a visual model into my lessons. Over the last decade of my teaching, I have watched students go from "I can't do it" to "I am going to try using this tool." I know that my own initial lack of self-confidence has not deterred me from becoming a better teacher of mathematics. I feel as if only recently I have been able to find the mathematician within. Now, I am ready to spread that self-discovery and knowledge to others.

Stories like Todd's are not unique. Women from all walks of life could relate episodes of their skillful navigation around mathematics course work during their years of schooling and their negative attitudes toward the subject. Some tell these tales with a twinge of regret, while others use humor to diminish the significance of these events. Because of mathematics avoidance, women can often be limited in their professional qualifications and may be barred from careers requiring mathematical knowledge.

The lack of mathematical knowledge does not affect just specific careers, but also maximum participation in our increasingly technological society. Innumeracy in the next century will be as dangerous as illiteracy was in this one. By *numerate* we do not mean knowing the basic arithmetic facts, but instead being able to solve novel problems, interpret mathematical data, and reason logically and effectively.

Although girls enter school more math-ready than boys, by the time they graduate high school females are outdistanced by males both in the number of higher level mathematics courses they take and the results of such critical tests as the SAT-Mathematics (American Association of University Women 1991). Women are much less likely to enter college as math-related majors or to later follow careers that relate to mathematics. In the critical years between primary grades and high school, what happens to girls that puts them at a math disadvantage?

Part of this change in girls' interest and confidence in mathematics during the period between fourth and eighth grade is due to a larger phenomenon. As girls progress through the late elementary school years and enter middle school, they are frequently seen as losing their daring nature (Brown and Gilligan 1992). They change from being outspoken ten-year-olds to young adolescents who respond with "I don't know" to most questions. Researchers report that adolescent females often lack a "hardy personality" (Ouellette and Puccetti 1983), a disposition that includes looking forward to changes and challenges, feeling in control of one's life, being responsible for one's own actions, and surviving unfavorable conditions.

Interestingly, these researchers also connect the characteristics of a hardy personality to successful problem-solving skills. Although the problem-solving skills they are discussing are not only mathematical in nature, these findings could be related to the fact that young females often lose interest in mathematics at the very same age. When female students do not have confidence in their ability to prevail in novel or challenging situations, their approaching mathematics problems with risk-taking behaviors seems unlikely. Bateson (1994) suggests that only by taking risks, do we learn and grow. "My own greatest resource as a teacher is the learned willingness to wing it in public, knowing that I will be faced with unexpected questions, some of which I cannot answer" (212).

Mathematics educators suggest that the kinds of mathematical problem-solving strategies we teach directly relate to the types of problems students face in the real world. We believe the reverse is true, as well. Girls who do not develop inner hardy personalities—who do not become "feisty females"—may not be prepared to tackle problem-solving situations. How can we help both build this strength and nurture these students to mature mathematically?

We undertook an action research project to probe the linkages between literature and mathematics that begin in the elementary school. In a two-year investigation we used books that featured rich stories of females who were risk takers, problem solvers, and who used their relationships with others to tackle difficult situations. Knowing that the really in-depth reading carried out in school settings often helps us think about our own character traits, how to face conflict, and ways to realize our dreams, we used these tales of characters who faced challenges to develop mathematics lessons. We found literature to be a fundamental way to present mathematics concepts and a medium that is integrally linked to the connected learning that is so successful with girls.

Our own research is steeped in the research of others who have looked long and hard at females' learning styles and the most successful methods for teaching mathematics. Therefore, this book meshes the knowledge base of researchers who have come before with the experiences in real classrooms of a university professor and three teachers. As the stories we use reflect proactive characters on a search for a greater understanding of self, we too are on a life-changing adventure.

Connected Learning

In our action research project we investigated one strategy for providing girls with examples of hardy female personalities through young problem solvers found in children's literature. These characters can act as springboards to mathematics lessons as teachers link these "feisty females" to mathematical activities. Children's literature provides a powerful context on which to build mathematical tasks and strongly influences the development of children's perceptions about their world. Through books we can find young, feisty females who face adventure bravely, make hard decisions, solve problems of their own and of others, and use their connections and network of relationships with other people as ways to both develop a sense of spirit and face new challenges. Pam Gilbert (1994) suggests that through repetition of story patterns and logic these ways of thinking "become almost 'naturalized' as truths and common sense" (10). Gilbert goes on to say, "We learn how to 'be' women or men, girls or boys, mothers or fathers, wives or husbands, sisters or brothers, aunts or uncles, grandmas or grandpas partly in response to the stories that we hear and participate in" (31). Therefore, the stories we read to children often become the essence of their reality.

This book-initiated reality is becoming increasingly important. In an age when children know television characters better than they know their own grandparents and cousins, positive role models are in short supply. Mary Pipher, the author of *Re-*

viving Ophelia, states that at about age twelve, girls abandon their "self" and trade it for what they believe to be a culturally accepted version. This is particularly frightening considering the advertisements, MTV videos, and characters commonly found on television situation comedies. In 1992, researchers from the American Psychological Association looked at the prototypical female as portrayed on television shows (Huston 1992; Pipher 1997). This female role model is young, beautiful, slim, and dependent on others. These are the very shows that children watch on an average of six hours a day. It is no wonder that girls idolize fashion models and are constantly concerned and frustrated with their appearance.

Television producers have found that girls will watch programs with male characters but boys are not interested in shows that center on a cast of female characters. Therefore, much of the programming emphasizes roles for boys. Even in the world of print we find the same pattern. When adult females are asked to recall books they were required to read during their school years, many are only able to remember books where the major character studied in-depth was a male (Fields 1995). Other research shows that the read-aloud preferences of elementary school teachers show a strong bias toward books with male authors and male characters (Smith, Greenlaw, and Scott 1987). In school textbooks girls will observe more than nine males to every one female in the illustrations they examine (AAUW 1991). Judy Mann (1994), in her book about growing up female in America, puts it this way:

> Little girls are so overwhelmed in this male culture that the story of little girls' lives is whispered, while the story of little boys' lives is shouted in books, movies, cartoons, and songs. We don't celebrate the wonderfulness of little girls nearly as much as we should. (19)

Unfortunately our educational institutions mirror society in the learning girls experience. The classroom assignments in schools often favor the male-oriented preference of "reporting" rather than the female-oriented style of "rapporting" (Tannen 1990). Although girls typically learn by making personal connections, in school settings they often face and are disadvantaged by separate, speedy, and silent learning (Gilligan, Lyons, and Hanmer 1990). These factors are often mentioned as parts of the "disconnecting" girls experience as they begin to lose their voice and change into the adolescents who claim that they "don't know."

The children's author Katherine Paterson suggests that girls use the characters in novels in a "rehearsal for living" (1996). This is a particularly potent insight as we examine what they have been reading and what has been read to them. As we approach the turn of the century, the students in our classes need to see in the media and read about a more diverse pool of models to act as mirrors so that girls in particular can see reflections of their own selves in the real world.

In addition, individuals with hardy personalities often come from families that encourage their members to go out and tackle stressful situations. In these changing times, we often see what once happened in families now extends to schools, with teachers often acting in ways that mentor girls and foster autonomous learning behaviors. In a book that advises parents how to make things different for their daughters, Bingham and Stryker (1995) suggest that "If she learns to tolerate anxiety and act anyway, she will be more likely to persist when she gets her first really tough assignment or fails her first test" (80).

Connected Teaching

Our goals in this action research project were to bring powerful mathematics to females, to help them develop a clear conceptual understanding and passion for the subject, and to nurture independent learning skills that will translate into all aspects of their lives. Fifty years ago, 75 percent of what students needed to know on the job they had learned by the time they completed high school. Now that figure is 2 percent (Barth 1997). The capability to be a lifelong learner who takes responsibility for constructing her own knowledge and skills is critical. By blending girls' interest in reading with mathematics, by resisting dominant story lines and instead taking steps to use characters with hardy personalities, by encouraging independence and risk taking, and by developing significant mathematics we hope to achieve these objectives.

Our work embraces females' special qualities and explores how instruction can be tailored to capitalize on their strengths. The connected teaching we suggest allows girls to weave together the various threads that compose their lives as well as the lives of the female characters in the literature. The students are encouraged to build upon their entire base of knowledge combining academic information and personal anecdotes rather than leaving their life stories out of the schoolhouse experience. Adapting instruction to meet their needs and learning preferences within the broader mathematical reform is paramount. Therefore, in this project, we consistently looked for ways to translate the research on gender and mathematics into workable classroom practices.

To develop a more gender-inclusive mathematics curriculum, different people have focused on different approaches. There have been three possibilities for change: girls themselves; teaching environment and practices; and the mathematics curriculum. Changing girls or changing their choices implies that what females are presently doing is deficient or inappropriate. Researchers at Smith College suggest through incorporating this model, in essence, educators gave girls courses in "remedial masculinity." We believe more realistic approaches are aimed toward teachers' practice, curriculum, and schools, as the broader cultural variables we spoke about previously are less within our control. Our intent and direction are to act more equitably with all students, girls and boys alike.

The current mathematics education reform movement initiated by the National Council of Teachers of Mathematics Standards is creating significant change in instruction. Our work with connected teaching practices honors the shift described in the NCTM Professional Standards for Teaching Mathematics (1991, 3), which suggests contrasting movements:

Toward	*Away From*
Classroom as mathematical communities	Classrooms as collections of individuals
Logic and mathematical evidence as verification	Teacher as the sole authority for right answers
Mathematical reasoning	Memorizing procedures
Conjecturing, inventing, and problem solving	Emphasis on mechanistic answer finding
Connecting mathematic ideas and applications	Treating mathematics as a body of isolated concepts and procedures

The research-based strategies we suggest as particularly successful with females must be guided by how the teacher views the nature of mathematics and how it can be learned. Adopting the techniques we speak of in isolation will not transform classroom practice. If manipulatives are used, for example, with a structured set of steps to manipulate materials, that learning will not compare to the learning achieved through student-driven exploration of concepts with the same resources. In the first situation the students are taught merely to memorize two procedures, one with materials, another with symbols. This rote use of materials leads to the lack of conceptual understanding we are trying to avoid. Also, traditional gender roles are reinforced if boys end up handling the objects while girls observe or record.

We generated mathematics lessons using books with hardy female characters and tested them in elementary multiaged classroom settings. We worked with mostly upper elementary students ranging in age from seven to eleven years old in classes with an age spread of at least two years. We believe the instructional activities are adaptable for children in grades two through seven. The activities, therefore, are open in nature, have multiple entry levels, and lend themselves to working with several age groups and ability levels. We focus on the early years so that a strong base of confidence, perseverance, and motivation can be established. The instruction also follows an in-depth approach to mathematics, one that avoids the recent description of the mathematics curriculum in the United States as "a mile wide and an inch deep" (TIMSS 1996).

Although we are interested in motivating students, we are not interested in activities that solely please children but do not give evidence that significant mathematics is being learned. We focus on four core mathematical areas that guide curriculum in mathematics in our state; they are number and computation, geometry and measurement, probability and statistics, and algebraic ideas.

The strategies discussed below reflect those suggested through research as essential to educational equity in mathematics education. The areas specifically developed include using various forms of communication, hands-on or manipulative materials, collaborative learning, authentic assessment models, connections, reasoning independently, and general strategies for encouraging females in mathematics and improving their confidence. In each chapter we describe how we used several children's books to develop instructional activities. We take a unit perspective rather than a lesson perspective, so although each chapter includes examples that highlight particular strategies, in most cases we are not exclusively dealing with one approach. Our classroom investigations of mathematical topics attempt to incorporate many of the components of a more connected teaching model.

Research discussed throughout the book often defines behaviors along specific gender lines, possibly leaving the impression that we believe all females are dependent and passive and all males are independent and active. Instead, we suggest there is actually a continuum, a full range of behaviors and actions with females and males distributed across the entire scope. Clearly, as many boys as girls will benefit from the support and suggestions we make and the exposure to multiple modes of knowing and models of understanding. (In contrast to some initial concerns, we found that the boys in the class were as interested in these stories as the girls, and each group made strides in achievement.) Our goal is to reach all learners in our mathematics classes. We do believe that students along the entire continuum will be relieved of the cultural and educational confusion that the quick answer is equal to the correct answer.

Our hope is that applying these instructional examples will not add work to your already hectic schedule. Rather we trust that you will look at the use of literature in new ways and see connections to the work you are already doing, so that your work in response to ours becomes one of refining ideas rather than of replacing ideas.

Works Cited

AMERICAN ASSOCIATION OF UNIVERSITY WOMEN. 1991. *Shortchanging Girls, Shortchanging America: A Call to Action.* Washington, DC: AAUW.

BARTH, ROLAND. 1997. "The Leader as Learner." *Education Week* 56 (March 5): 42.

BATESON, MARY CATHERINE. 1994. *Peripheral Visions: Learning Along the Way.* New York: HarperCollins.

BINGHAM, MINDY, and SANDY STRYKER. 1995. *Things Will Be Different for My Daughter: A Practical Guide to Building Her Self-esteem and Self-reliance from Infancy Through the Teen Years.* New York: Penguin Books.

BROWN, LYN MICKEL, and CAROL GILLIGAN. 1992. *Meeting at the Crossroads: Women's Psychology and Girls' Development.* Cambridge, MA: Harvard University Press.

DRABBLE, MARGARET. 1975. Interview, *The Guardian* (London), 5 August, p.16.

FIELDS, TEESUE. 1995. *Positive Role Models in Children's Literature.* Paper presented at the Annual Conference for the Association of Women in Psychology, Indianapolis, IN, 4 March.

GILBERT, PAM. 1994. "'And They Lived Happily Ever After': Cultural Storylines and the Construction of Gender." In *The Need for Story*, edited by Anne Haas Dyson and Celia Genishi. Urbana, IL: NCTE.

GILLIGAN, CAROL, NONA P. LYONS, and TRUDY HANMER. 1990. *Making Connections: The Relational World of Adolescent Girls at Emma Willard School*. Cambridge, MA: Harvard University Press.

HUSTON, ALETHA C. 1992. *Big World, Small Screen: The Role of TV in American Society*. Lincoln: University of Nebraska Press.

MANN, JUDY. 1994. *The Difference: Growing Up Female in America*. New York: Warner Books.

NATIONAL COUNCIL OF TEACHERS OF MATHEMATICS. 1991. *The Professional Teaching Standards*. Reston, VA: NCTM.

OUELLETTE, SUZANNE KOBASA, and MARK C. PUCCETTI. 1983. "Personality and Social Resources in Stress Resistance." *Journal of Personality and Social Psychology* 45: 839–50.

PATERSON, KATHERINE. 1996. Quoted in "Words Under the Words: Learning to Listen to Girls," by Maureen Barbieri. *Voices from the Middle* 3 (1): 33–40.

PIPHER, MARY. 1994. *Reviving Ophelia: Saving the Selves of Adolescent Girls*. New York: G. P. Putnam.

———. 1997. Conversation with Karen Karp. 13 March.

SMITH, NANCY, M. JEAN GREENLAW, and CAROLYN J. SCOTT. 1987. "Making the Literate Environment Equitable." *The Reading Teacher* 40 (January): 399–407.

TANNEN, DEBORAH. 1990. *You Just Don't Understand: Women and Men in Conversation*. New York: Ballantine.

TIMSS. 1996. *Third International Mathematics and Science Study*. Washington, DC: U. S. Department of Education. National Center for Educational Statistics.

1

Seeking Stories

Our culture, as well as others over the centuries, discourages risk taking in females. Females are frequently the objects of "rescuing" when difficult or dangerous situations arise and, in some cases, when they are merely in discomfort. They are encouraged to be helpless. As Bronwyn Davies writes in her book *Shards of Glass*, girls understand that they must "correctly constitute themselves as girls" (136). In many cases, this means that to be "good girls" they must show that they are inactive and powerless. When girls believe the only alternative to the message "wait and be rescued" is "be tough, deal with it, or pull up your bootstraps," the lack of support inherent in the alternative is often considered more unpleasant than staying in a passive mode and waiting for help.

Clearly, it is critical to move away from this model, but changing long-held thinking is not easy. "We will never effectively change the way we raise girls unless we also change the way we raise boys, and we will never alter the outcome for most girls until we change the way boys think of girls" (Mann 1994, 15). Women must be raised in a culture that doesn't focus on how girls look or what they can do for others but that emphasizes who they are and what they can do. Students need to read about characters that model healthy gender roles.

All-Important Decisions

Selecting books that deal with the issues of helping oneself by one's own initiative or by a web of connected relationships and support from others is neither a simple nor unimportant process. Finding books about strong female characters is not easy. We frequently use books that have already been reviewed for their literary value in places like *The Horn Book Guide* and *Language Arts*, a journal of the National Council of Teachers of English. Two recent and exciting resources are a new book by Katherine Odean, *Great Books for Girls*, which contains an annotated bibliography, grouped by reading ability and category, of more than six hundred female-friendly books, and *Let's Hear It for the Girls: 375 Great Books for Readers 2–14* by Erica Bauermeister and Holly Smith. In addition, we have benefited from the careful scrutiny of some publishers and vendors who examine their offerings with an eye to females' presence and role in the story. They only offer titles that show females as strong characters. These include the Feminist Press, Carolrhoda Books, Just Girls: Books That Celebrate Girls, Books for Our Children, and Chinaberry Press. At the end of this chapter there is information to help you access these and other resources.

Looking at potential selections in the bookstore is not always a successful route unless you have the opportunity to read the book in its entirety or the author has had a successful record of books about hardy female characters. Many expensive mistakes along our way convince us that a time-consuming review process is in fact a savings.

The most memorable blunder we made was purchasing a book that on first glance appeared very promising in every way. The story told about a young girl who came from a long line of exceptional women, five of whom were captured in a family portrait in the book's very first illustration. The image included the girl with this daring group—from her great grandmother in bicycle-racing gear to her mother in motorcycle garb. As the plot progressed, the young heroine becomes a member of a male soccer team. Only after reading the story do you find she made the team because one of the uniforms was too small for a boy. Even when she leads the team to victory and saves the day, in actuality she wins the game by her shorts falling down and continuing the competition in her underpants. The other team's players become so disoriented that they quickly find themselves at the point of defeat. Sad to say, this book is not an exception. We found many examples of children's literature that included stories of girls waiting for a prince, craving romantic entanglements, in dire need of rescue, or passively observing as boys are taking the lead. Fortunately, more and more authors are writing books with positive role models for females. Remember to be thorough in selecting your texts since the conclusion of a promising story may merely reinforce a conventional lesson.

Children's literature can transport young students to other worlds, places where there are possibilities and options that can be tried on for size. Like many quality books, these stories can be transformative and give girls an opportunity to test new versions of themselves.

Many of the books we selected are picture books, which was a strategic decision. Although some of these are easy reading for the upper elementary students, they often tell powerful tales in very efficient ways with vivid visual clues that can be more easily integrated with mathematics lessons. They are also very effectively presented in two relatively brief readings, with the second reading scheduled just prior to mathematical linkages.

We have used both fictional and factual tales that invite students to respond thoughtfully, examine fresh perspectives, investigate all aspects of a story while enabling them to be more understanding of themselves, their peers, and their world. We do not mean to suggest that there is a single meaning to be gleaned from any of the books we recommend. As in mathematics where there are multiple ways of looking at problems, in literature there are multiple ways of examining plots and developing story lines into mathematical journeys.

Telling Tales

Children's literature can be used for a variety of purposes in the classroom. First, we celebrate its use for pure enjoyment and personal connections. Reading to children creates an intimate bond between children and their teacher that invites the sharing of emotions and ideas. What better place is there than in the security of a classroom for a group to laugh in delight together, share sadnesses, and question the world around them? Good literature explored together is a rich experience. Having children discover the wisdom in each book is a powerful way to foster discussions that delve into right and wrong, dreams and goals. Literature is a vehicle for teaching strategies, concepts, ideas, points of view, and sharing values through characters.

When we introduce a piece of children's literature, we make it the focal point of our instructional time. We gather in a smaller section of the room where students are comfortable and the stage is set for the storytelling. Before reading the book, we share background about the author and the illustrator and read the dedication aloud. Many times that information alone creates a personal bond between the author and/or illustrator, and the audience. We routinely examine the cover of the book and make predictions concerning the story line based on the illustration or the title.

Examining the copyright date offers some mathematical activity as we identify the book's birthday. The children are always interested in how old the book is, comparing it to their age and the age of other recently read books. When we have several versions of the same story (as with the tales of Cinderella or Little Red Riding Hood), we like to place them in order from oldest to youngest.

In each case, we read the books in their entirety with no interruptions. In the children's initial interaction with the text they are encouraged to open themselves to the literary experience, then later they can focus on the interpretation. After the children experience the story and the illustrations, we customarily begin a "grand conversation" about the literary elements such as characters, plot, theme, problem solving, and message. We also reexamine our initial predictions and compare them to the way the story actually evolved. The children discuss the characters for their qualities and personalities as they make connections between the characters' lives and their own.

After we finish reading, we may use a story web to record the students' ideas about the book's message. Another technique we use to think about the book that links to analyzing data mathematically is to give each student a small sticky note and ask them to write the problem that was resolved in the story. We then place these on the board in a bar graph, as we group the problems according to categories the students develop, or we place them in a Venn diagram as we compare the story we are currently reading to another we have read previously. Students can visually compare their ideas to their classmates' to see if they identified thinking that was similar or unique. In the early part of the year this helps students, particularly girls, who are hesitant to share orally in the large group setting. Using this approach they can share an idea through a nonverbal format and gain confidence.

We go back and forth through the book as children mention certain text or illustrations in making their points. Sometimes we revisit and reread portions that we found particularly satisfying. As the children comment, we have collected their thoughts along with the title and author of the book and the date on flower blossoms made of construction paper. These blossoms are then hung on a vine that continues to grow, inching its way across the classroom wall. This visual display of the books we have read throughout the school year becomes a growing graph that acts as a record and time line of our reading progress.

To encourage more comfortable discussions and risk taking, the class is divided into small groups for a more nonthreatening environment. The literature circles that develop provide more response opportunities and greater active participation for students who are sometimes intimidated by conversations in front of the whole group.

We do not introduce the books with an overt discussion of the story being about a strong female. Instead, we allow the discourse to take its own path. The children often stretch the ideas beyond the initial focus of the author. Like us, they begin to look at these books in different ways—seeking the mathematical connections and embroidering on the fabric of the story.

Good children's literature thus becomes a starting point for great mathematics instruction and mathematics assessments. The mathematics lessons begin with the second reading of a book. We find that children love hearing good literature more than once if it is read with excitement and enthusiasm. Many times they capture new ideas that they missed the first time through, and often they read familiar phrases along with the reader. During the second reading, the children are asked, "What mathematics do you find in the story?" Then the mathematical wisdom the children discover in the story is shared. The focus in the second reading on the mathematics encourages the students to search for mathematical ideas including vocabulary, problem solving, patterns, change, and skills in real-world use through the book setting. Students become quite adept at finding examples of mathematics that may very likely escape your view or explanation. Occasionally the link between the story and the mathematics is a stretch, but frequently there is a genuine real-world connection.

The value of this second reading is to have the children consider the story from another perspective as well as for another purpose. When we first started using literature in the mathematics classroom, we felt more comfortable using selections with obvious mathematics themes such as *Grandfather Tang's Story* and *Alexander Who Used to Be Rich Last Sunday*. But many of those books were about men and boys, and we wanted to expand the reach to include females. So, using literature with more subtle connections to mathematical ideas became a challenge. We are continually

14

surprised and amazed by the number of ways children notice mathematics that we had not thought about. This is also a very good approach to reinforcing the process of brainstorming. All answers are accepted. These mathematical conversations invite children to piggyback on each other's thoughts, which we find generates a great deal of energy around mathtalk. Part of the children's thinking has involved forecasting what the teacher has already discovered as the mathematical concept or idea, and making predictions about the task ahead.

Having read the story and discussed the mathematical wisdom, we then introduce a prompt for a mathematical investigation or task. Of course, some of the initial prompts we develop in advance of the reading are altered or even traded for other activities by the children's discussion. The prompts connect the story lines about the hardy female characters with a problem-solving challenge. The tasks are purposely constructed to be open-ended to allow for multiple answers and multiple strategies.

The development of the prompt is a very creative process that works to engage students in meaningful mathematical thinking with connections to the characters. Some might pose the question "Why not just bypass the book and move directly to the activity to save time?" Our research shows that by having a book and a character as a point of entry, you can always refer to the character or problem when assisting the students as they forge forward in their own problem solving. The prompt is an initial catalyst to unify the group in their purpose and approach.

The prompt is put on an overhead transparency and the group reads the task together. The discussion in this introductory phase provides an opportunity to observe whether students are aware of the criteria for the outcome. We often suggest possible strategies, tools, and resources, and fix a workable time frame. The students are then given their own copies and begin conversations at their tables. We find it is critical to move quickly around to each group at this point to discover which avenues they are beginning to pursue. With some children, being able to go back and reread a section of the book will refresh memories and spark additional ideas so the book is left on the chalkboard ledge for easy access.

Since we most frequently take a unit approach rather than a lesson approach many prompts require several class sessions. The students seem to need the table talk and the chance to test the use of different materials and strategies to come to a solution. Talking about the hurdles they face, sharing successes along the way, questioning each other on alternative possibilities are all part of the process. When given the time, the level of thinking and reflection deepen significantly.

Works Cited

DAVIES, BRONWYN. 1993. *Shards of Glass: Children Reading and Writing Beyond Gendered Identities*. Cresskill, NJ: Hampton Press.

MANN, JUDY. 1994. *The Difference: Growing Up Female in America*. New York: Warner Books.

Children's Literature

TOMPERT, ANN. 1990. *Grandfather Tang's Story*. New York: Crown Publishers.

VIORST, JUDITH. 1978. *Alexander Who Used to Be Rich Last Sunday*. New York: Macmillan.

Cinderella Stories

HOOKS, WILLIAM H. 1987. *Moss Gown*. New York: Clarion Books. Set in southern United States.

DELAMARE, DAVID. 1993. *Cinderella*. New York: Simon & Schuster. Set in Italy.

JACKSON, ELLEN. 1994. *Cinder Edna*. New York: Lothrop, Lee & Shepard Books. Set in the United States.

MARTIN, RAFE. 1992. *Rough-faced Girl*. New York: Scholastic. A Native American retelling.

STEPTOE, JOHN. 1987. *Mufaro's Beautiful Daughters: An African Tale*. New York: Scholastic.

VUONG, LYNETTE DYER. 1982. *The Brocaded Slipper*. New York: HarperCollins. Set in Vietnam.

YOUNG, ED. 1982. *Yeh Shen: A Cinderella Story from China*. New York: Philomel Books.

Red Riding Hood Stories

ERNST, LISA CAMPBELL. 1995. *Red Riding Hood: A Newfangled Prairie Tale*. New York: Simon & Schuster.

MCKISSACK, PATRICIA. 1986. *Flossie and the Fox*. New York: Dial Books for Young Readers. Set in southern United States.

YOUNG, ED. 1989. *Lon Po Po: A Red Riding Hood Story from China*. New York: Philomel Books.

Information Resources

Books

BAUERMEISTER, ERICA, and HOLLY SMITH. 1997. *Let's Hear It for the Girls: 375 Great Books for Readers 2–14*. New York: Penguin.

ODEAN, KATHERINE. 1997. *Great Books for Girls: More Than 600 Books to Inspire Today's Girls and Tomorrow's Women*. New York: Ballantine Books.

Journals and Magazines

The Horn Book Guide: This guide, which comes out semiannually, reviews every new hardcover trade book for children and young adults, of which there are more than 2,000 a year. Write The Horn Book, Inc., 11 Beacon Street, Suite 1000, Boston, MA 02108. 1-800-325-1170.

Language Arts: This journal is published eight times a year by the National Council of Teachers of English for its members. There is a section called Bookalogues: Talking About Children's

Books, which reviews literature from picture books to chapter books. Write them at Language Arts, NCTE, 1111 W. Kenyon Road, Urbana, IL 61801-1096. 1-800-369-6283.

New Moon: A Magazine for Girls and Their Dreams: In 1993, a mother of teenagers began publishing this bimonthly magazine as a source of information and a forum for stories aimed at girls ages 8–14. Now the magazine is managed and edited by a staff of twenty young girls. The articles frequently discuss females who have taken on challenges and helped others. Children's literature is often mentioned in articles and it is specifically reviewed in a section called Books for Girls. To subscribe write to New Moon Publishing, P.O. Box 3587, Duluth, MN 55803 or call 218-728-5507.

Teaching Tolerance: This is a journal published twice a year at no cost to educators. The articles covering a range of subjects revolve around the issue of diversity in the classroom. One section, Teaching Tools, evaluates children's literature. You can write (on school stationery) for a free subscription to: Teaching Tolerance, 400 Washington Avenue, Montgomery, AL 36104. Or fax: 1-334-264-3121.

The Bulletin of the Center for Children's Books: This is a monthly journal that contains full-length book reviews written by experts in children's literature. You can subscribe by writing, The University of Illinois Press, 1325 South Oak Street, Champaign, IL 61820-6903. 217-333-8935.

Publishers and Book Distributors

Books for Our Children: This catalog features children's literature about African Americans. It contains annotated listings for fiction and nonfiction. You can send for a catalog by writing, Books for Our Children, Inc., 513 Manhattan Avenue, New York, NY 10027. 212-316-1255.

Carolrhoda Books: Lerner Publishers offers this collection of books, which are divided into categories such as "Trailblazers" and "On My Own" Books. The address is: Carolrhoda Books, 241 First Avenue North, Minneapolis, MN 55401. 1-800-328-4929.

Chinaberry Book Service: With absolutely engaging and well-written reviews, this catalog is a reading experience in itself. The reviewers really capture the story and the emotions in each tale—making decisions on female-friendly literature easier. Send for its catalog by writing Chinaberry Book Service, 2780 Via Orange Way, Suite B, Spring Valley, CA 91978. 1-800-776-2242.

Feminist Press: This press has been in existence since 1950. While its primary focus is on adults, it does have a selection of books for children and young adults. Its address is The Feminist Press at the City University of New York, 311 East 94th Street, New York, NY 10128. 212-360-5794.

Just Girls: Books That Celebrate Girls: There are five catalogs printed each year, and each issue includes books with reading levels from ages 4–14 on the contributions of real women to the history of the world and about girls who are adventurers, heroines, decision makers, leaders, achievers, problem solvers, and strong, curious, confident and active participants in everyday life. Write Just Girls, P.O. Box 34487, Bethesda, MD 20827. 1-800-465-5445.

Web Sites

The Children's Literature Web Guide: (http://www.ucalgary.ca/~dkbrown/)
This site is a guide to Internet resources related to children's literature. It includes discussion groups, award-winning books, teacher resources—including lesson plans and even home pages of many authors.

Vandergrift's Special Interest Page: (http:/www.scils.rutgers.edu/special/kay/kayhp2.html)
Kay Vandergrift is a faculty member in the library at Rutgers University. She has developed a rich web site that shares ideas and information about children's literature with some components related directly to books about girls. The site is driven by her desire to match curriculum and children's learning styles with literature.

2

Talking with Words, Pictures, and Numbers

In the past, people and story plots often tried to shield girls from life's harsh realities. "We treated them like princesses when we wanted them to be presidents" (Shuker-Haines 1994, 76). Females were sent a clear message that to be loved they must stay "little" and sweet and helpless (76). In many cases this message was carried further by encouraging girls to become agonizingly afraid of people being angry with them. In response to that fear, many girls bend over backwards to please—and never learn to speak their mind (Roberts 1994, 76). Although girls are often rewarded in schools for their ideal, docile behavior, in reality the world rewards assertiveness and speaking up as critical qualities on the road to success.

Females, more frequently than males, need to be invited to express their opinions. Adults must resist the urge to rescue girls as they attempt to shed their "rule follower" image and instead permit them to make mistakes and discuss errors. Sometimes when our expectations manifest society's often-demonstrated belief that girls should be mild-mannered and proper, we inadvertently discourage risk taking.

Females who are quiet, conscientiously do their work, and do not cause trouble in the classroom are easily and effectively ignored (Milligan, Thomson, and Ashenden & Associates 1992). Yet researchers who have studied how females learn best suggest that valuable educational experiences for females often take place in the form of conversation (Belenky, Clinchy, Goldberger, and Tarule 1986). Listening and talking are critical in making sense out of new material and information. While girls have traditionally been supported as good listeners, it is also essential that they construct and contribute ideas orally to the dialogue. Students who flourish in an environment where students build on one another's ideas through verbal exchanges often have difficulty with a narrow, one-right-answer approach to mathematics. Therefore we try to focus on the mathematical thinking rather than a lockstep search for solutions. Students, particularly females, need to openly talk about their discoveries and listen and react to the thinking of others. They must be encouraged to discuss, negotiate, and debate.

Mathtalk

In our project, we often tell girls to "Be confident" as we encourage them to share and justify their thoughts. We know that through the work of Nancy Austin and others who look at helping girls succeed in mathematics that "teachers must ask early and often for learners' voices" (1996, 33). Through our active listening and questioning we are able to allow knowledge to emerge as students express their thinking and raise concerns about areas that need further clarification. Our job becomes facilitating the conversation as the teacher and students think critically together.

Rather than using the traditional "doubting" mode, we incorporate a "believing" mode (Elbow 1973). The doubting mode suggests that the teacher does not believe what the individual is saying and that the student must prove otherwise. The believing mode assumes that theirs is a valid point, and students are asked to elaborate and provide rich detail to their idea. Children in the believing mode often identify their own misconceptions and make corrections in their work as the conversations continue. This is more affirming than the teacher confronting inconsistencies in students' thinking with an attitude of doubt and disbelief. Through this method students become more independent and autonomous as they come to understand the mathematics and refine their thinking on their own.

There is much support for the practice of incorporating autobiographical methods in teaching (Grumet 1988; Miller 1987). Students savor stories about people, and building in their own human experience makes the material come alive. Curriculum builders need to regard females' experiences as the foundation for educational thought and practice. Thus, students' personal stories are becoming powerful tools in the curriculum.

Belenky, Clinchy, Goldberger, and Tarule's work (1986) emphasizes the potency of "quiet observation, listening to others, and personal experiences that women can relate to" in the learning process. They suggest that these elements are prerequisites for the most efficient learning of abstractions. This is important when trying to understand the discipline of mathematics, as abstraction is a key to the conceptualization of mathematical thoughts. The mechanism of sharing mathematics in the written form seems to be a dynamic teaching alternative.

For years, the assumption has been that females have strengths and learn well in areas that emphasize both talking and writing. If this assumption is indeed true, then writing about mathematics events or thinking may be an important mode for communicating ideas for females and one that should be actively pursued in the teaching of mathematics.

Writing Mathematically

Mathematics writing encompasses a variety of purposes. Marilyn Burns points out that writing "encourages students to examine their ideas and reflect on what they have learned. It helps them deepen and extend their understanding" (1995, 13).

William Zinsser (1988) suggests that writing is a way to work yourself into a subject and make it your own. Another purpose of writing is the link to a model of connected teaching, by enabling students to develop their voice and to focus on the process not just the answer.

As girls discuss and brainstorm what they understand about a problem, writing can be beneficial to them as an organizer. Using a "What Do I Know?" chart we adapted from KWL and the work of Rachel Griffiths with four structuring queries, we found writing responses to these questions is particularly helpful as students search for solutions. First, the students are asked "What do we know?" This question provides students with an opportunity to share ideas about what the problem is really asking and to examine the problem for clues that might assist in choosing a strategy or finding a solution. The discussion may center on sorting the valuable from the useless information within the problem. Recording this thinking creates a bank of information that can be a useful resource during the problem-solving processes.

The second question the students consider is "What puzzles us?" At this point students contribute any thoughts or opinions about what they find problematic. Are there any components that we don't understand? Do we need to reread the problem again? Is the problem like any we've seen before? Is there anything in real life that we've encountered that could guide us? Everyone becomes involved in helping to erase misunderstandings that others may have.

The third question we use is "What patterns do we see?" As students examine the information before them, they discuss numerical patterns, patterns in the language of the problem, or patterns that link to possible strategies. They record these repeating elements as they begin searching for a path that might identify a solution.

The fourth question the students ponder is "What strategies that we know might help us solve this problem?" Here students brainstorm ideas for approaches and tools. We attempt to focus on the thinking they have become familiar with through solving problems. In some cases we encourage students to recognize a problem as similar to one they have seen before. This frequently leads to a previously successful plan of action.

The "What Do I Know Chart?" is also an effective tool to use with students after they have completed the problem solving and prior to beginning their writing. Many times problem-solving activities span several class periods. By using the "What Do I Know Chart?" before writing, the ideas, processes, and strategies can resurface and become the forefront of students' thinking. We put a strip of paper with the chart headings (What do I know?, What puzzles me?, What patterns did I see?, and What strategies did I use?) on the chalkboard. Then we fill our pockets with markers and a small pad of notepaper. As we walk around and have students share their problem-solving experience, we ask them to write their reasoning on notepaper and tape it to our chart. Contributing their own unique ideas to the chart keeps students engaged. This activity moves the ownership from the teacher to the children. In addition, it brings out some of the girls who are not generally eager participants in a large-group setting. We make a concerted effort to get each student to have one or more of their ideas on the chart. This may take time, but it is well worth the investment to see students rethinking and analyzing what happened.

The chart creates an idea bank from which students can borrow as they write about their own solutions and strategies. The chart is especially effective for students who are not strong auditory learners, have attention deficit disorder, or short-term memory difficulties. You rarely hear "I don't know what to write" and, because they can refer to a collection of ideas, their reflections have more insightful connections. By using the categories, "know," "puzzles," "patterns," "strategies," the writer offers more than just the answer and a computation.

Writing in mathematics is used not only to extend and even deepen children's thinking, but also to help them form, rethink, and refine their ideas. As they do rethink them, we always ask them to include their first ideas in their writing. We do not want students to erase their first attempt, or redo the paper so their original thoughts are lost or ignored. Recognizing the value of the initial thinking to the evolution of the whole process is critical to problem solving. We often compare this written record of dead ends to the work of real mathematicians. In many cases the sharing of unsuccessful thinking has led to major breakthroughs in the field. Students are intrigued by tales of the time-intensive and complex struggles of even the best math minds.

Sometimes mathematics writing is useful in a journaling format. The children may be asked to reflect on an experience where they used mathematics or saw mathematics being used by someone else. Students may simply express their thoughts on what they learned in class that day, how another student chose to solve a problem, or the challenges of being a mathematics student. Children need to realize early on that mathematics writing is not simply a method for recording the answer to a problem in words; it is a chance for reflection and expression about their processes and a chronicle of their growing understanding.

Early in the year, Lauren's entry reflects on what she might choose to teach students for a week if given the opportunity to be a math teacher (see Figure 2–1). She referred to children's literature, computational mathematics, rounding, estimation, and fractions.

Students are somewhat apprehensive about writing in a mathematics class if they have never been asked to do so. With time and experience, good modeling by the teacher, peer conferencing by other students, and reading aloud works of others, students gain confidence in their own writing. Sharing mathematics writing with the whole class and in small groups gives students a chance to experiment with their thinking in front of their peers. In the process of sharing they may extend their knowledge, enrich it with the help of their friends, and make it truly part of their mathematical thinking.

The following books share some ways we use communication through words, pictures, and numbers to develop mathematically literate students.

If I was the math Teacher
for one week...

I would teach about those crazy
numbers. That were mengend in the
book Math Curse. They Kind of
go like this 1,10,2,20,3, and 30.
Thats as far as I know. I would
also teach about multiplication,
divion, and fractions. I would
also like to do something like
I would have a big Jar and fill it
up with candy and have the
every body guss how many are
in there.

fractions

4/8

FIGURE 2–1 *Excerpt from Lauren's journal*

Growing Mathematical Ideas

City Green, by DyAnne DiSalvo-Ryan, shares a real-world experience about living in a large city and working cooperatively. Marcy, the young girl in the story, decides to make a difference in her neighborhood by transforming a cluttered vacant lot into a community garden for everyone to enjoy. She enlists the help of all the people in the neighborhood, but in the process of building the garden, she develops a special friendship with a grumpy old man who once lived in the dilapidated brownstone that sat on the now vacant lot.

Before we could finish reading, the class had their hands fluttering in the air wanting to share the mathematical wisdom of the book. The thoughts and reactions were thrown into the discussion at a rapid pace. Some of the children's mathematical connections included: How was the garden divided into sections? How long would it take to tear down a building? How long does it take for plants to grow? How tall do sunflowers grow? How many buildings are on one city block? What is the height of city buildings? What is the cost of real estate? and How many families live inside a brownstone? In addition, many students immediately recognized the concepts of area and perimeter as they related to the garden.

From our discussion we sent a team of students to the technological investigation center to see if a CD-ROM database search or the Internet could reveal the actual dimensions of a brownstone building in New York City. While some students were researching, other students remained in the classroom examining seed packages for a variety of vegetables and flowers so data could be collected from the back of the packet to calculate plant size and the area needed for planting.

When the investigation team returned with limited data on the actual size of a brownstone, the children decided to use logical reasoning instead of trying to find the information through a database and come to consensus on what might be a reasonable measurement for such a structure. In an effort to create an actual representation of the vacant lot, they used the one-foot-square floor tiles in the classroom to walk off and mark house-sized plots. They agreed that the dimensions would be between nineteen and thirty feet wide and twenty and forty-five feet in length.

A mathematical prompt was introduced to the children that allowed them to solve the problem from multiple entry points. Students who still needed manipulatives such as color tiles or cubes to represent a square foot of garden had that option, while others worked directly with grid paper to create a model of the garden.

The prompt for *City Green* asked students to design a representation of a garden. This scaled drawing should have the garden divided between Marcy and five of her neighborhood friends. In the written portion of the task students needed to explain why they chose the manipulatives that they did and clearly explain the mathematics in their work. After the prompt was introduced, the children began the mathtalk that enabled them to internalize what they were to do and to begin making initial decisions on how they would start.

Here are some of the initial comments made in the discussions:

STEPHANIE: Ms. Allen, do all the friends get the same amount of space?
MS. ALLEN: Well, Stephanie, what are your thoughts about that?
STEPHANIE: I think to be fair they all need the same exact space.

KEVIN: I don't think that Mr. Hammer and Mr. Bennett will want the same amount of space. They're old and they probably cannot work that hard.

MAGGIE: Yes, but we should at least give them a chance to have an equal part.

MS. ALLEN: Children, you should make that decision. Each of you can decide if you want the shares to be equal or not. That is your choice, as you consider the information you have.

KENNY: Do we use all the space for the friends or can we leave space for the other neighbors?

MELISSA: Can we plan to have a picnic area for all the neighbors so they can sit and look at the garden?

MS. ALLEN: Both of those are interesting ideas that you can consider. You need to think about the mathematical consequences of sharing the vacant lot. Let's reread the prompt and begin talking at your tables about how you want to solve the problem.

The activity time continued at the tables with discussions about appropriate divisions of the land, how much area was needed for the different parcels, and space required for a variety of garden plantings. Students continued to use the floor tiles, color tiles, or centimeter cubes as reference points to model and explore the areas they were designing. During this time, other individuals asked them questions about their process of subdividing their garden plot. Some children still insisted that the garden be divided into equal parts, while others maintained that Old Man Hammer would not want an equal share because of the difficulty of working the section. Others liked the idea of leaving an area for a picnic table that all the neighbors could enjoy. At first several children estimated that the area for the picnic table should be two feet wide by two feet long. They thought it appeared large enough in comparison to the sections they were marking off for six individual gardens but they weren't sure. Others quickly initiated a discussion as to whether or not anyone could sit in that space, much less have a picnic table in an area that size.

MS. ALLEN: Sarah, how could you find out if the area you chose for a picnic table would work?

SARAH: I could make that space on the floor to see how big it really is.

JOSH: What if we use the square tiles? We could count them out and lay things around it to look like a picnic table.

Sarah agreed with her group, but she did not yet have a firm understanding of what they were asked to do. She expressed that she was sure that a four-square-foot area would accommodate a table with benches around it. Laying rulers around the four-square-foot area revealed the exact size of the proposed picnic area. Sarah was surprised at the results. Returning often to the visual model of the space allowed students to mentally capture the reality of their plans and better understand their scale drawings. Many designs were changed after examining the corresponding floor tile representations. Some students were able to make decisions concerning walkways through the garden, bench areas for observing, and picnic areas for relaxing after seeing the reality of the space.

The gardens continued to go through several peer revisions. Some revisions were made because the choice of materials was not as efficient as students had originally thought. Other revisions were made as the students moved from needing concrete models to being able to think more abstractly. In the process, students worked cooperatively to make suggestions and help each other find appropriate manipulatives, create models, and design scale drawings that would lead to accurate solutions. Students wrote about the problem and about their problem-solving process as part of the ongoing work for their mathematics portfolio. One girl wrote, "The strategy that I used was logical reasoning. It would not be logical to give half of the garden to one person and distribute the other half between several people." She also included her mathematics: "I decided that my brownstone building would be 29 feet in length and 23 feet in width. I gave each gardener a 9×5 garden. This gives each gardener 45 square feet in total garden area. I left a one-foot walkway between each garden" (see Figures 2–2 and 2–3 for another child's response).

Marcy's hardy personality led her to find a solution to a local problem by working cooperatively with others. She saw an opportunity to replace a vacant lot with a green space. The community's example of group problem solving provided the class with an enriching project involving geometry and spatial sense.

Picture Perfect Data: Going Glyph Crazy

Glyphs are pictorial representations whose features represent data on a particular subject. These simple illustrations are a way to communicate using pictures, much like hieroglyphics were used as a language in ancient Egypt. In the same way these childmade graphics can tell tales about their creators and their experiences. Students are provided with a menu of choices from which they choose symbols that describe their thinking. Just like numerical graphs, the picture data can be used to make observations and generalizations.

We used glyphs in our mathematics instruction in the past but did not fully recognize their potential. Glyphs allow students to interpret data using real-world experiences and connections to literature. Incorporating the literature component gave us a larger variety of information to gather and a way to connect the personal to the mathematical. The interest of the children encouraged us to have glyph making a monthly event.

Since our glyphs are sources of information for others as well as for ourselves, the class enjoys displaying them in the hallway for passersby to interpret. Therefore, to enable visiting classes to accurately read the stories the students are telling through pictures, a key to the symbols is always included.

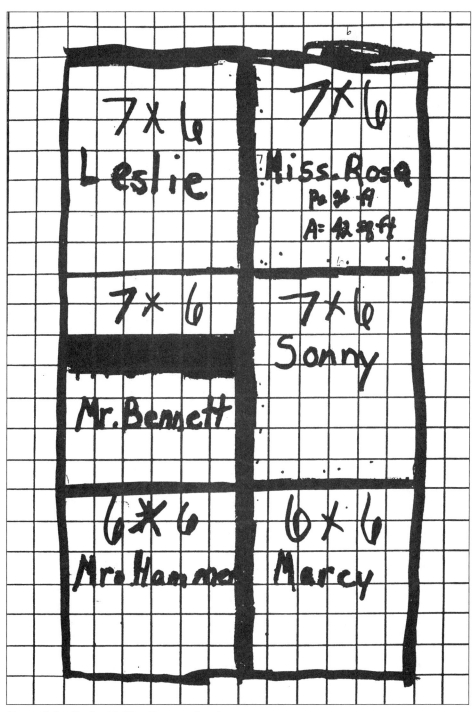

FIGURE 2–2 *Stephanie's City Green garden picture*

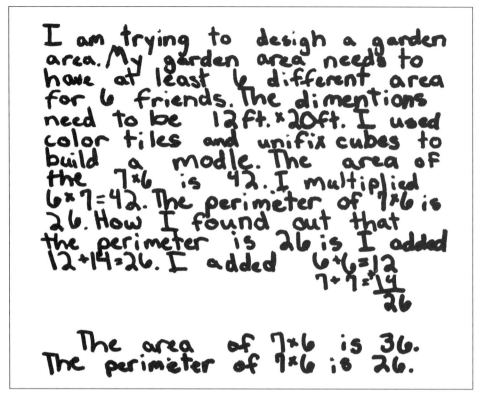

I am trying to desigh a garden area. My garden area needs to have at least 6 different area for 6 friends. The dimentions need to be 12ft.×20ft. I used color tiles and unifix cubes to build a modle. The area of the 7×6 is 42. I multiplied 6×7=42. The perimeter of 7×6 is 26. How I found out that the perimeter is 26 is I added 12+14=26. I added 6+6=12 7+7=14 26

The area of 7×6 is 36.
The perimeter of 7×6 is 26.

FIGURE 2–3 *Stephanie's garden description*

A Close-Knit Family

The Faraway Drawer, by Harriet Diller, is a touching story about a young girl's daydreams. She creates these mental images based on the carefully knit designs of people and places that are woven into the sweaters crafted by her great-grandmother. Each sweater inspired the girl to envision a different story of things to come. Through the use of a vivid imagination, the little girl dreams of the future and finds that the images she predicts might become real.

Not long before locating the book *The Faraway Drawer*, we had been envisioning ways to get students to think about their future. This story and the faraway pictures on the sweaters became the appropriate avenue. To continue our investigation into glyphs, we decided to use a sweater as the base for the data collection.

The Faraway Drawer task asked the students to design a sweater using a glyph key that would record predictions for their "faraway" future. The symbols students could choose corresponded to questions that asked in which state or country they might live, the planet they would most like to visit, the number of times they might make house changes in their lifetime, and the type of career they might choose. Each different symbol or color would represent a specific response to a question. For example, the color of the sweater they chose would indicate which planet the child wanted to visit.

The students used the following key to select features for their glyphs.

What planet would you like to visit?

Red = Mars	Yellow = Mercury	Orange = Saturn
Blue = Venus	Green = Jupiter	Pink = Other

Where will you live in the future?

Cut out the state you would like to live in from the map. If you wish to live in another country, look at a map and draw the shape.

How many times do you think you will move?

Draw a crow for each time you think you will move.

What type of career will you pursue? (Use the alphabet design on your sweater.)

Professional (doctor, lawyer, teacher, nurse) = PPPPPPPP
Service (restaurant worker, salesperson, painter, mechanic) = SSSSSSSS
Entertainment (athlete, dancer, singer, musician) = EEEEEEEE

Once the students selected their sweaters' color, they began working on developing their designs (see Figure 2–4). In our conversations about specific career goals and the categories they might fit into, we realized we forgot to ask the students to predict which job category would appear most often. In hindsight, that data should be collected.

Most frequently, we post the glyphs and ask students to look for patterns in the data. This time, we decided to take a different approach to the model of analyzing the data holistically in a picture form. To unravel the meaning of the data, we assigned each table the task of collecting all the information for one category, preparing a graph, and presenting the synthesis to the group. At one point, Beth came up to the front of the room and said, "How can I have counted a total of seventy-three crows when there are only twenty-seven people in the class?" We asked her to restate in her own words the question she was answering and the information she was collecting. She told us she wanted to find out how many times each person would move in the future, so she needed to look at the crows on each sweater and count them. Then, we asked her how she knew if the class members were predicting that they would make one move, two moves, or three moves in their lifetime. Beth put her hand to her head and said, "That's what I did wrong. I have to go back and look at how many each person has and group them rather than count each bird." She walked away all smiles. A few moments later, John approached us with the exact same dilemma. Interestingly, Beth was close by and she said, "I'll help him." She turned to John and as they walked away said, "I did the same thing, John."

The glyph of the month graphs provided a more detailed assessment of how students can interpret the collected data. The graphs showed the students' growth in identifying and labeling axes and varying the range of the scale to fit the data onto

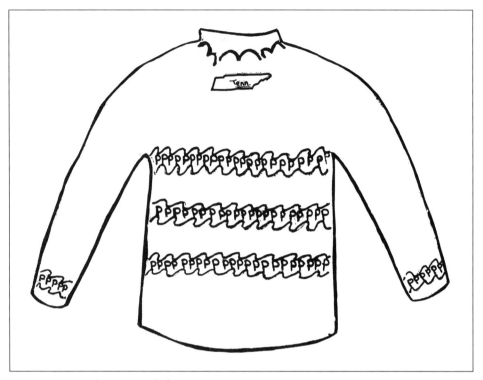

FIGURE 2–4 *Caitlin's sweater glyph*

the grid paper. Students moved from simple bar graphs to more complex double bar and circle graph representations.

As the students' analyzed their own futures through the glyphs, they continued to think of how someday they might play a role in their own grandchildren's lives. In linkages made back to the book, students told stories about their grandparents that we realized could lead to even further data collection. The conversations around the books and the ensuing mathematical activities helped students learn more than we had anticipated. When children do not consider mathematics by the heading on their textbook page, they are not encumbered with the thought that today will be strictly the study of "fractions." This allows concepts to emerge. Through the background students bring to the classroom, they can see beyond curricular boxes and approach mathematics more holistically and authentically. The connections they freely fashion are rich and filled with meaning.

An Olympian's Trials

Although March is Women in History Month, every month is celebrated that way in our mathematics class. We make a special effort to seek out a literature book that will give us a historical perspective of both women's contributions and mathematical knowledge in the process. *Wilma Unlimited: How Wilma Rudolph Became the World's Fastest Woman*, by Kathleen Krull, tells the childhood trials of Olympian Wilma Rudolph. In the story she exemplifies the very perseverance that must be fostered in our young female mathematicians. When we read this story, you could have heard a pin drop. They were mesmerized by Wilma's life. The thoughtful discussion that emerged centered on Wilma's ability to visualize herself winning. Several students shared their own experiences and deliberations on the mental element of sports. Then as always we asked, "Where is the mathematics?" The children quickly identified the length of the races Wilma ran, the fifty-mile bus ride to the hospital twice a week, and her weight of four pounds at birth. They had many questions about polio, which Wilma successfully battled as a child. It was explained that polio was an epidemic in the 1950s that affected many families and that this medical nightmare ended with the discovery of a vaccine. The story naturally guided us into a real-world data collection about the students' early years. The prompt for *Wilma Unlimited* asked the students to create a glyph that recorded data about their childhood. These data might include their birth weight, birth month, time of birth, childhood diseases they endured, and the summer Olympic medal they would want to win. That night they were sent home with an assignment that included interviewing parents or other family members to find out facts about their birth and whether they had childhood diseases such as chicken pox, measles, or mumps. Each child was given a pattern of a running shoe and a menu that contained the elements of the glyph.

The completed running shoe glyphs were posted on the wall, which gave the impression that they were racing across the front of the room. The students were given time to collect data on one or more categories and construct their own graph. Immediately, they noticed that there were very few green and yellow dots, which were used to represent childhood diseases. Why did so few people have measles and mumps? The students were challenged to find out. The question led them to Wilma's battle with polio. Why did we not include polio as one of the childhood diseases on the glyph? Several students made immediate connections, realizing the discovery of vaccines had an impact on the data.

Having worked the week before with mode, mean, and range, they noticed the range of birth weights. Everyone was intrigued by the fact that one girl in the class was born prematurely and weighed only two pounds. At first she had many skeptics who said she couldn't have been that little. On the other end of the continuum was Michael, who, at eleven pounds, by far had the greatest birth weight. To help them see this range, we created a two-pound "baby" and an eleven-pound "baby" by using one pound bags of rice wrapped in a small blanket, which they could hold and compare. The students were surprised by the difference.

By placing the completed glyphs on chart paper, we stored them for future reference. As the year progressed and students grew in their ability to interpret data in graph form, they revisited the information for additional interpretations. This cycling back to familiar information enriches the experiences in writing and justifying conclusions.

Brainstorms

An important way for girls to learn to communicate mathematically is through instruction that involves building mathematical models. These models depict a physical representation of an abstract mathematics concept. For true understanding students need to talk about the connections between the concrete and abstract. We tried this approach with the book *My Head Is Full of Colors* by Catherine Friend. This is a wonderful story that leads to the creation of a physical model of a fractional whole.

The plot centers on young Maria who wakes each morning to find her head literally filled with books or colors or animals or people. As she actually has these things on her mind, she spends the day focusing on her strengths and knowledge in each particular area. Maria showcases her talents and abilities as she reveals what she knows about each of these subjects. Primary children eagerly want to share the ideas that fill their heads, and so that brought us to a dynamic lesson on fractional parts of a whole while investigating the children's unique abilities and interests.

After several months of daily calendar activities that included some work with fractional concepts we presented a challenge to a multiage class of six- and seven-year-old students. After the second reading of *My Head Is Full of Colors* the children discussed Maria and all her extraordinary head-filling topics. The book discussion pointed out that over the course of the story Maria had four different ideas that occupied her thinking. We then asked the children to identify the topics that absorbed their attention. First we had them return to their tables to draw or list in their math journals those topics that they thought of frequently, knew a lot about, or captured their interest. One student asked, "Should we have just four thoughts like Maria or can we have more?" We responded that they could have exactly four or fewer or more. After an energetic writing time, the students came to the Talking Circle and shared their ideas. The Talking Circle is derived from the customs of Native Americans in the Southwest who gather together in circles to explain their viewpoints on particular situations and events. Everyone is to listen attentively and try to understand the other person's perspective. We frequently use these gatherings for a variety of purposes.

We created a list on the board that included all the ideas that the children had brainstormed. The students helped reorganize the chart into tallies by category that corresponded with their thoughts. The list was fairly large, and after everyone had responded the students began analyzing the data and explained what statements they could make about the responses. Ideas included "Only one person likes to think about frogs," "Six people have books in their head," and "Lots of kids have school in their heads."

The following day we shared with the class a paper-plate model of Maria's head. The model was made by using two paper plates, which were attached by cutting slits in each disk from the edge to the center (radius) and sliding them together. They then could be turned to reveal portions of the plate underneath.

We asked the children what they noticed about the model. The students recognized that the colorful flowing hair and the face on the top plate looked just like Maria. Then as we rotated the outside paper plate a quarter of a turn we revealed that beneath was one-fourth of Maria's head, filled with colors. We made a second turn to reveal one fourth of her head filled with books. Two more turns revealed one fourth filled with people, and one fourth filled with animals. We demonstrated the process a second time before pulling the two paper plates apart to show the "whole" back plate divided into fourths with each section covered over with magazine pictures or drawings of Maria's important thoughts. Students immediately noticed that the plate was divided into fractional parts—in this case fourths. The students talked about how they could divide their own "heads" into fourths or eighths or halves. Most of the students decided to divide their heads into fourths because their small group discussions led them to understand that even if they had four different topics, they would still have enough room to draw or glue several pictures. This artistic decision showed that students understood that as the denominator increased the equal parts actually decreased in size. They wanted room for pictures!

The students worked collaboratively to fold the paper plates, accurately dividing the whole into halves and then fourths. Group dynamics became a side issue as children remembered the ideas of their classmates and tried to assist them in their projects. While scouring pages of magazines for their own work, they would also look out for pictures that fit their classmates' lists (see Figure 2–5).

A third day gave students an opportunity to share their paper-plate images of what's on their mind and to reflect on the work in their journals. We asked the students to study their models and then write three or more statements that described the mathematics. Eight-year-old Lauren's head shows that it is filled with pasta, dogs, writing, and science. Her statements included, "2/4 of the thoughts in my head are filled with things I like to do at school," "1/4 of my head is filled with things I have to take care of," "1/4 of my head is filled with my favorite thing to eat," and "1/4 of my head is filled with doing investigations."

Another day one of the students mentioned that she could describe the class's original brainstorming list with fractions. The discussion that followed included an interesting discovery. Intuitively it seemed like the denominator used to describe the list should be twenty-fourths to represents the number of students in the class. But the students were unsure. We let the conversation take its own course and, rather than interfere with their thinking, we asked questions like "Do you agree with Tom?" and "What do you think about Lisa's idea?" With some debating, students concluded the denominator would actually need to be larger because everyone in the class had more than one choice.

The same lesson can easily be adapted to older students by using a circle graph

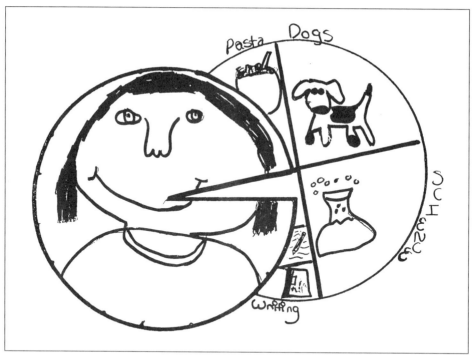

FIGURE 2–5   *Lauren's head, full of ideas*

with a key to show what each section of their "heads" contained. The lesson might also be a successful "getting to know you" activity at the beginning of the year to encourage inclusion while simultaneously assessing students' general understanding of fractions. The connections made between the concrete fractional model and the abstract mathematical concepts were made through the dialogue and the written communication.

The stories in this chapter lead our young mathematicians through discussions and written records of strategies, constructions of models, utilization of technology to locate information, and building ownership of a whole "head full of ideas." Through these activities students develop skills in communicating mathematically, a critical avenue for females' grasp of the important ideas in the discipline.

Works Cited

AUSTIN, NANCY. 1996. "Emerging from the Past: Reclaiming the Mathematician Within." *Focusing on Learning Problems in Mathematics* 18 (1, 2, 3): 32–40.

BELENKY, MARY, BLYTHE CLINCHY, NANCY GOLDBERGER, and JILL TARULE. 1986. *Women's Ways of Knowing: The Development of Self, Voice, and Mind.* New York: Basic Books.

BURNS, MARILYN. 1995. *Writing in Math Class*. Sausalito, CA: Math Solutions Publication.

ELBOW, PETER. 1973. *Writing Without Teachers*. London: Oxford University Press.

GRUMET, MADELINE. 1988. *Bitter Milk: Women and Teaching*. Amherst: University of Massachusetts Press.

MILLER, JANET. 1987. "Women as Teachers/Researchers: Gaining a Sense of Ourselves." *Teacher Education Quarterly* 14 (2): 52–58.

MILLIGAN, SANDRA, KAREN THOMSON, and ASHENDEN & ASSOCIATES. 1992. "Listening to Girls." Report of the consultancy undertaken for the Australian Education Council Committee to Review the National Policy for the Education of Girls in Australian Schools. Carlton, Victoria.

ROBERTS, KATELIN. 1994. As quoted in Franny Shuker-Haines, "On the Home Front." *Parenting* (April): 75–76.

SHUKER-HAINES, FRANNY. 1994. "On the Home Front." *Parenting* (April): 75–76.

ZINSSER, WILLIAM. 1988. *Writing to Learn*. New York: Harper & Row.

Children's Literature

DILLER, HARRIET. 1996. *The Faraway Drawer*. Honesdale, PA: Boyds Mills Press.

DISALVO-RYAN, DYANNE. 1994. *City Green*. New York: Morrow Junior Books.

FRIEND, CATHERINE. 1995. *My Head Is Full of Colors*. New York: Hyperion Books for Children.

KRULL, KATHLEEN. 1996. *Wilma Unlimited: How Wilma Rudolph Became the World's Fastest Woman*. Orlando, FL: Harcourt Brace & Company.

3

Hands-On, Minds-On, and Hearts-On

When a child is born, the most commonly asked question is "Is the baby a boy or girl?" Depending on the answer, people will make decisions as to what the child's room will look like, how the child will be dressed, and what playthings they will purchase. Even when adults are given an opportunity to play with a young baby, they actually engage in different activities with the child, playing with them more vigorously or gently depending on whether they were told the infant was a male or a female (Will, Self, and Datan 1976).

From the time they are little, males are frequently supplied with objects that encourage moving, building, and taking things apart and putting them back together. They are apt to be taught at a very young age how to catch a ball and hit a target. On the other hand, females are commonly given toys such as dolls, which involve more passive play revolving around relationships with people and practicing roles in the family. As a result females frequently have less practice in activities involving spatial sense.

It's not surprising that males prefer activities involving the use of objects or active games whereas females look for activities in which people skills and relationships are practiced (Leder 1990). Therefore, girls are more likely to lack spatial and part-whole experiences in handling concrete objects, which often leaves them at a distinct disadvantage in both mathematical and scientific work.

As the world moves toward more technology, boys are again favored. The games and programs that are developed for computer use are geared to enticing males to the sales counter. Violence, fast action, and rough sports are the common threads amongst the most popular software. Even the name of the major handheld hardware, Game-Boy, suggests who will be playing. The few games developed with girls in mind focus on designing clothes for Barbie or mall shopping. What message is being given?

When girls do not have the opportunity to dig into the learning event, use computers, or handle lab equipment, they experience a separate and distancing experience. Instead, they need to have hands-on and minds-on contact with the instructional activity for a relevant, significant learning event. Females can gain the feeling of control over mathematics by playing and messing around with mathematical objects and ideas. Connecting visual models to concepts helps all students as they develop mathematical structures in their minds. The power of visual representation cannot be overemphasized.

More essential than using manipulatives, however, is the connected teaching that links the models to more abstraction. This can be accomplished through ties to personal experiences. Personal scenarios brought into the instruction by a teacher or students help construct lasting meaning and knowledge.

Hearts-On Learning

Belenky et al. (1986) suggest that as females develop into constructivist thinkers they also change from passive to passionate knowers. An awareness of her mind's workings is critical to a female's well-being and confidence. Therefore, it is not surprising that many well-educated women who can successfully solve mathematics problems are still uncomfortable with mathematics because they are unsure of how formulas "work." They may not grasp the underlying concepts because in school speed, not understanding, was prized.

Females need to integrate their passions into their intellectual life—care and feeling are connected to "hearts-on" learning. Girls tend to use their "self as an instrument of understanding" (Belenky et al. 1986, 152). The linkages among the hands, mind, and heart are where manipulative materials come in.

Using manipulatives is advantageous for females in developing their understanding of mathematical concepts, according to Patricia Campbell (1995). Campbell goes on to state that "Manipulatives are perfect in getting females to take part in the learning process." In addition to improving conceptual understanding with the incorporation of manipulatives, the active involvement of female students in class with concrete materials improves their attitudes and confidence toward mathematics (Fennema and Sherman 1978). In fact, using manipulative materials as physical representations of mathematical ideas in instruction is seen as a potent tool for building the conceptual framework of all students.

As teachers we need to recognize how girls have been influenced by society and to provide opportunities for positive experiences with mechanical and spatial activities. Manipulatives are helpful thinking tools; in our project we constantly tried to use innovative ways to connect them with math concepts.

Stitching Lives Together

The Rag Coat, by Lauren Mills, is the story of a charming young mountain girl named Minna. Minna needed a winter coat before she could go to school. When the "quilting mothers," who meet at Minna's house each day to sew and share stories about their families, offer to make her a coat from scraps of materials, Minna carefully chooses pieces that are connected to the best stories. Although she loves her new coat, the children in school make fun of her rag coat. Minna develops a strategy to deal with this situation that ends up helping her establish relationships with her peers.

After reading this book to the class, the students talked about the mathematics involved in making quilts. Rather than start with cloth we began with wallpaper pieces, which allowed exploration of the geometrical shapes, reflective symmetry, and rotational symmetry found in a nine-patch square.

The students used a nine-patch composed of nine two-inch squares in a three-by-three array. There are endless possibilities for variations on a nine-patch pattern, so in preparation for paper quilt construction we used an overhead and overhead tiles. Using square tiles of several colors, students explored several basic designs. By seeing the variations on the overhead, they discovered and discussed the lines of reflective symmetry. Were they horizontal, vertical, or diagonal? How many lines of symmetry did they see? This exploration also introduced the use of triangles when we drew the diagonal line on several of the nine-patch patterns.

The students then experimented with the paper pattern and pencils to see what kind of design they wanted to carry out. Some decided to have reflective symmetry in their patch, so with great determination they sought out pieces that would make this possible. After locating a wallpaper pattern they liked, they traced around a two-by-two-inch template and then cut out their squares. Before gluing down the pieces, they positioned a mirror along possible lines of symmetry to help them determine if there was vertical, horizontal, or diagonal reflective symmetry. One child wrote about his design, "There is a line of symmetry in my patch. We can tell this by using a mirror. We look at the reflection, and then lift the mirror up and look under. Then we see if I can see the exact same thing as the reflection." This became an eye-opening lesson in which students learned that reflective symmetry is a precise mirror image, not just a repeating pattern.

Because new language was needed to discuss other patterns the students noticed, we brought in the vocabulary of rotational symmetry. Students held their quilt patch upright and giving it a 90-degree turn clockwise tested whether their original design still looked exactly the same. Some students found that on each turn they still had the same design thus finding rotational symmetry. Others found they had to give their patch two turns (or 180 degrees) before it looked the same again, while others could not find any rotational symmetry in their piece. Students who had found reflective symmetry were surprised when they did not have rotational symmetry. Students discussed whether there was a relationship between having one kind of symmetry and the other.

Then the students suggested a quilting project of their own. After a discussion, it was decided that each student would design and quilt their own nine-patch square out of cloth. Just as Minna did in the story, the children sought fabric scraps at home that had special meaning to them. The class revisited the skills involved in making a quilt from creating a design on paper, to cutting out fabric from square and triangle patterns, threading a needle, hand stitching, quilting, and edging.

Each child started with nine four-inch squares. When some children wanted to use triangles, this brought up the dilemma of how to mix squares and triangles when sewing. Students had to invent a way to make triangles fit exactly next to the squares after stitching them together. After experimenting and comparing paper squares and triangles, they determined that some adjustments would be needed. They found that if they wanted to mix triangles with squares they had to create a larger triangle to accommodate the need for extra seam allowance. They found that to add a one-half-inch allowance all the way around the edges meant a change to each side dimension of an additional inch. At first they were quite surprised that they needed so much more material if they chose to use triangles in the pattern.

The children worked diligently on their projects at school and home for a period of about two weeks and were as proud of their finished product as Minna was of her winter coat. As students looked at the final quilt piece, they spontaneously discussed how much of each fabric pattern made up their whole quilt square. We took this opportunity to extend a simple comment into a specific look at fractional parts and percentages. One girl wrote about her quilt square suggesting,

> I see lots of math in my piece and you can see it too. The two blue squares are $^2/_9$ of the whole piece of quilt. The black and white pieces are $^5/_9$ of the whole. And the blue and teal pieces are $^2/_9$ of the whole. The percentages for the black and white pieces are 56 percent. The percentages for the two blue pieces are 22 percent. And the percentages for the teal and blue pieces are 22 percent.

The children also examined classic quilt patterns through a book called *Eight Hands Round: A Patchwork Alphabet*, by Ann Whitford Paul, which looks at traditional quilt designs. Another book by the same author, *The Seasons Sewn*, tells about the seasons of the year in patchwork. Using these books as models, the culminating event was to give a name to their quilt square and share in writing a story that revealed all the mathematics in their quilt, how the design was named, and what they learned from the project. Like Minna, they realized how their problem-solving strategies were important in facing real-life situations.

Positively Brave!

Emily Arnold McCully's *Mirette on the High Wire* and Carol Saller's *Bridge Dancers* introduce us to two characters who overcome fears to display their strong personalities. Mirette lives at the turn of the century in a Paris boardinghouse run by her widowed mother. There she comes upon Monsieur Bellini, a retired high-wire walker, crossing the courtyard on air. "Her feet tingled as if they wanted to jump up on the wire beside Bellini." Mirette finds out from others that Bellini was once known for his many daring feats and was called "the man with nerves of an iceberg." At first Bellini discourages Mirette from attempting the high wire, but Mirette ignores his warning and continues practicing and falling. There comes a day when a courageous Mirette takes a chance and helps Bellini, an action that leads to the beginning of a great partnership. Finally, she shows Monsieur Bellini what she has learned, and he says, "Most give up. But you kept trying."

In the book *The Bridge Dancers*, Maisie's hardy personality is overshadowed by an older sibling named Callie, who enjoys taking risks. Callie teases Maisie by walking, twirling, and leaping out on the old footbridge, which is a shaky old skeleton of ropes and boards. Eventually Maisie is faced with the frightening situation of having to cross the bridge to get help for her sister.

The characters in both of these stories had to take steps to overcome fears. The books led to an activity that involved working with integers. The model of a high-wire or rope-bridge number line with positive and negative numbers can be used to explore the operations of addition and subtraction. At first we had students use a number line on the floor so they could role-play Mirette and Bellini while reacquainting themselves with the addition and subtraction of positive numbers on the continuum. The addition of positive addends was familiar and therefore a good starting point. We knew that when negative numbers were added to the mix that the familiar would rapidly take on unfamiliarity, so we had students take their time and record patterns of movement and behavior at each juncture. The concepts eventually would be manipulated through mental images so the models needed to be carefully built. Then, we posed a problem for the students by asking them, "Since subtraction is the opposite of addition, what would be a good way to show this on the number line?" After acting out some actual problems they decided that like the movements in the story they would walk backward to show the subtraction. They identified walking forward to the right to represent addition of a positive number and walking backward to the left to represent subtraction of a positive number. As a reminder we placed a marker at the "landings" at the end of our classroom number line, the one to the right reading "positive" and the one to the far left reading "negative." Students then created stories about Mirette or Bellini on the "high wire" (or Maisie and Callie on the rope bridge) and showed the corresponding equations. For example, Bellini is standing five steps away from the center of the tightrope. Mirette is at the center when she takes three steps toward Bellini. Now how far would he need to walk to get to her position? Then they acted out the problem and represented the story in symbols, in this scenario $5 - ? = 3$. Although these problems may seem too simple, these number sentences provided patterns that became the basis for more complex thinking.

In the next activity, the students constructed a paper number line and selected Mirette or Bellini as their puppet (see Figure 3–1). Through exploration and investi-

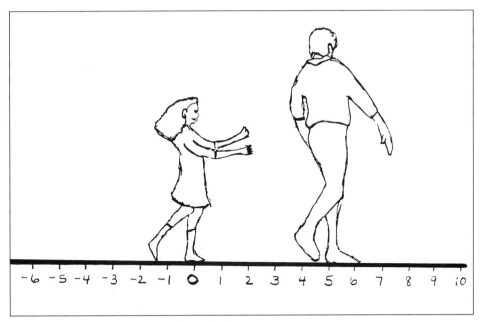

FIGURE 3–1   *Mirette and Bellini on the number line*

gations that included going back to the role-playing, students were able to figure ways that negative numbers needed to be used to represent stories they were creating. They found that when adding a negative number you face left on the number line (toward the "negative" sign) and walk forward. For subtraction of a negative number they faced left on the number line and stepped backward. The intention was not to make students dependent on a model, but to have them explore relationships between real situations and numbers, thereby taking out some of the mystery and confusion.

Mirette and Maisie led us to some active problem solving. McCully has written a sequel, *Starring Mirette and Bellini*. This book could be used later in the year to revisit this concept. There are many mathematical concepts that can be developed using these models, numbers lines, and literature. Primary students can use a similar approach and look at addition and subtraction with intervals of ten between the number line delineations. Rounding can be presented as a way to get Mirette or Bellini back to the nearest "landing" at any given point on the high wire.

A Penny for Your Thoughts

The Hundred Penny Box, by Sharon Bell Mathis, is a timeless story of how oral histories bridge generations. The book introduces us to Great Aunt Dew who is one hundred years old. She has an old box with one hundred pennies that are her springboard to stories. She reaches in, looks at the year the penny was minted and tells an event in her life that happened that year. Great Aunt Dew successfully faced many struggles in her one hundred years. We found mathematical connections that would engage our third- and fourth-grade students in investigating their own lives and looking at pennies with a more personal lens.

Our first activity was to have students create a penny collection with a penny for each year of their lives. They were asked to write a story or state, like Aunt Dew, meaningful events that happened in their life during the year each penny was minted. These personal penny time lines gave us an opportunity to compare our lives in a mathematical way. The students brought in their projects and they shared their stories. There was a mixture of posters, penny books, pennies attached to time lines, and even a penny quilt. Casey constructed an eight-inch-by-twelve-inch quilt. She had ten small pockets, each of which held a penny. Each pocket was decorated with a symbol to represent the event she shared for that year. She writes, "1993—The red cross stands for my first time in the emergency room, because a rock split open my knee." After our sharing time, students commented on what they saw:

> JUNE: I think it was interesting to find out about the past. I hope that I have great grandchildren who will count my pennies so I can tell them something special that happened that year.
>
> RAPHAEL: You can keep track of your life without just counting the years. It kind of organizes your life.
>
> ERIN: My parents told me things that I forgot that I did when I was little.
>
> BLAIR: I liked learning more about other people. Since I just moved here this year, I liked learning about all of you. It was very helpful to me.

The next phase of our penny investigation had the students examine the displays and look for patterns. They were all able to see similarities in their birth years. We saw that we had more eight-year-olds in our class. We saw that over half the class had picked important events that involved pets. The students also noted that they remembered times they got hurt. Many students identified trends in the age when they learned to ride a bicycle.

Some children remarked that while making their time line, it was easier to find some specific-year pennies than others. In response, we asked students to bring in a pocketful of pennies for our next activity. We reminded them that we wanted pennies that were being used now, not ones from collections like Great Aunt Dew's. The students brought in their pennies and talked about ways they could find which year had the most pennies. The students suggested that they would construct a graph. We asked them to count the total amount they brought to school and record that number in their journal. Also, we asked the children to make some predictions:

- What year penny will appear most often?
- In what year was the oldest penny minted?
- How many pennies will be found from the current year?

The students shared their predictions with their neighbors and the class proceeded. Next we asked students to sort their coins by the year they were minted and record the year and total of pennies from that year in their journal. While they were sorting, we walked around and recorded the years from the coins. With this information we labeled thirty cups with a year date and lined them up on the chalk tray. We reminded the students about the story and how Great Aunt Dew's penny collection was contained in a single box. The students placed their coins in the cups, which were sorted by year. When all coins had been collected, we gave the students one of the cups and asked them to double-check that all the coins in their cup were from the same year.

We had prepared a large grid on which the students could place the coins. Starting with the oldest coins, students set the pennies in a vertical line by year. Initially, they wanted to stack them into bars for the graph, but after twenty-five pennies the towers tipped over. The students predicted the pennies would be in fairly equal amounts over the span of years. Surprisingly, the greatest amounts on the graph were from the last five years. We then asked the students to write three questions that could be answered by looking at the graph. Many questions involved counting the numbers of pennies in a given year. By modeling other questions that involved comparing, some students did write more complex examples. A student asked "Even though we are not finished with the 1990s, why are there more pennies from the '90s than the '80s?" Another posed the question, "Why is it so hard to find pennies from the years my parents were born?" Some children wondered, "Are the same number of pennies made each year?" Then we asked the children to exchange papers with a neighbor and try to research or generate an answer to their partner's questions.

Infinite Possibilities

The main character in *Come Away from the Water, Shirley*, by John Burningham, is certainly a feisty individual. Left alone to devise her own fun at the beach, Shirley uses her creative imagination to build ships and battle dangerous pirates. In her virtual adventure she becomes the heroine by making choices for herself and showing her strength.

As the group discussed the book, Linda Fay noticed that "The page on the left side of the book has real-life things on it, and the right side has pretend or fantasy things on it. Like the parents can really sit on the beach in the chairs, but Shirley can't fight pirates." Andrew chimed in, "The pages are a pattern: parent page, Shirley page, parent page, Shirley page." The class reviewed some of the scenarios in the story and made decisions about whether those were activities that Shirley might actually carry out in real life. The lesson quickly moved to thinking about what was certain and impossible. Would it be certain that Shirley could do it, would it be impossible, or would it be somewhere in between? Using components of the story, the children were asked to talk about the probability of the events occurring. They easily selected situations that were impossible, but then the students debated about others which were more or less likely to happen.

Then we moved away from the context of the original tale. Taking a long strip of cash register tape and affixing it to the chalkboard, we created the Line of Possibilities. We drew a horizontal line in the center of the tape with two ending points. We asked the students, "If we wanted to place the words *certain* and *impossible* on the line, where should they be written?"

EVAN: I think the words could go on either side. Why would it matter?

TAMARA: Since the line is like a number line, we should put *impossible* on the left end like we do when we put zero on the left. That means there is no chance that something could happen. We would put *certain* at the other end to show it really will happen. It is certain.

MS. ALLEN: Listen to this question as I'm going to have someone come and place a mark in a place on the Line of Possibility that will show how they answered the question. "How likely is it that you will not be in school on Sunday?"

JACOB: I'd place it on *certain*. No one will come to school because we don't have school on Sundays.

MS. ALLEN: "How likely is it that you can walk from our school to the state capitol before it gets dark today?"

TERRY: I'd put it on the *impossible* side. I know I can't walk that far that fast.

MS. ALLEN: "If last month I brought my lunch ten times and I bought the school lunch ten times, how likely is it that I brought my lunch to school today?"

WESLEY: Well, it's either yes or no. So it's in between *certain* and *impossible*.

MS. ALLEN: Use some of your mathematical vocabulary and tell me how we would describe what is in between *certain* and *impossible*.

BRETT: That's like half and half . . . or fifty-fifty . . . or even 50 percent! It's like a zero is no chance, and certain would be like a one because it's a whole chance, and then the middle would be half a chance for happening and half a chance for not happening.

MS. ALLEN: What does that mean when I am talking about bringing my lunch to school?

BRETT: It means that you might bring it to school, but you might not. There are equal chances.

MS. ALLEN: We could then say that it is equally likely that I would bring my lunch, and also equally unlikely that I would bring my lunch. On the Line of Possibility where would I then place my mark?

TAMARA: It would go in the center.

Each student is then given an eighteen-inch-by-one-inch strip of white paper for an individual line.

MS. ALLEN: We are going to create individual Lines of Possibility out of this paper. I want you to mark the *impossible* point and the *certain* point, and then I want you to mark the *equally likely/equally unlikely* point. How can I tell where to mark that?

CATHARINE: We can fold it in half to find the center.

MS. ALLEN: The first question asks, "How likely is it that you wear shoes to school each day?" On your Line of Possibility place a number "one" for the first question in the spot where you thing your answer falls. The second question asks, "How likely is it that an alligator spoke to you on the way to school?" On your Line of Possibility place a number "two" for the second question in the spot where your answer falls.

Now I want to pose another question to you that is not on your sheet. What if I asked, "How likely is it that the person sitting next to you has a peanut butter sandwich in his or her lunch bag today?"

HEATHER: I know he loves peanut butter sandwiches and has them all the time, so I know I'd make my mark close to certain.

MS. ALLEN: But that is an interesting question for me. I do know she has peanut butter sandwiches more than she doesn't have them. How can I use the Line of Possibility to show my neighbor's chance of having a peanut butter sandwich?

ANNA: You can put the mark on the spot halfway between *equally likely* and *certain*.

MS. ALLEN: We named the center point *equally likely*, but we also named it *fifty-fifty*, *50 percent*, and *one-half*. What name could we give to the mark that Anna located?

HEATHER: It could be named three-fourths because it looks like the line is divided into fourths, and then the other mark would be one-fourth.

DREW: Then we could name the one-fourth also as 25 percent and the three-fourths also as 75 percent.

MS. ALLEN: If we answered the peanut butter question and made our mark at the 25-percent spot, what would that tell everyone about the person's likelihood of having a peanut butter sandwich?

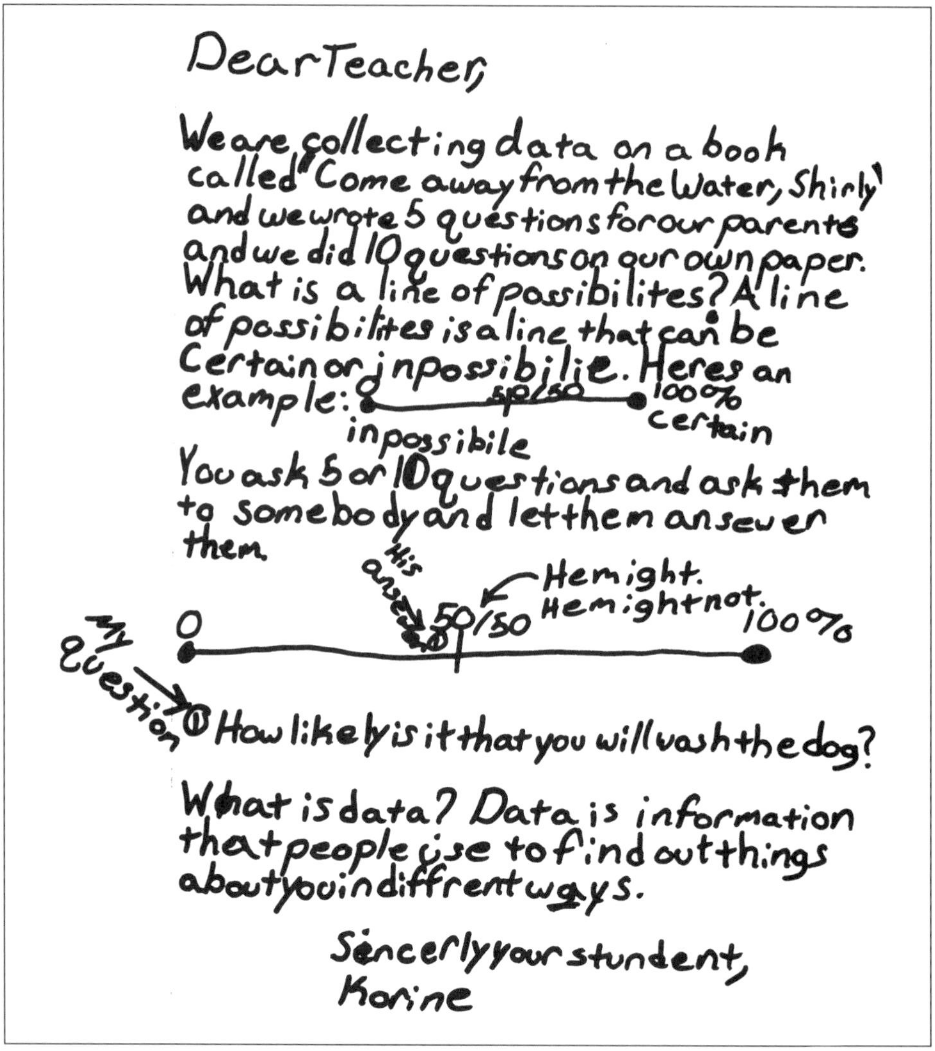

Dear Teacher,

We are collecting data on a book called "Come away from the Water, Shirly" and we wrote 5 questions for our parents and we did 10 questions on our own paper. What is a line of possibilites? A line of possibilites is a line that can be Certain or inpossibilie. Heres an example:

0   50/50   100%
inpossibile   certain

You ask 5 or 10 questions and ask them to somebody and let them answer them.

his answer →
my question →

0   50/50   He might. He might not.   100%

① How likely is it that you will wash the dog?

What is data? Data is information that people use to find out things about you in diffrent ways.

Sincerly your stundent,
Korine

FIGURE 3–2 *Korine's work on the Line of Possibility*

BRETT: It means that you don't often have it, but you do once in a while.

MS. ALLEN: How can we add marks for the points at 25 percent and 75 percent to our Line of Possibility?

ANDY: We would fold it back in the center, and then fold it again and we would have fourths or the 25-percent and 75-percent spots.

MS. ALLEN: Now you are ready to answer the other questions. You need to decide where your mark will be placed to answer each question.

After students completed several questions, they were asked to find an empty space on their line where no answer fell. Then they had to design a question for themselves that could be answered by placing a mark in the blank spot on the line.

As a follow-up and a chance to get parents involved in this probability activity, students created a second Line of Possibility and a set of five questions that they could use to survey their parents. Modeling had to take place over and over to help the children formulate their questions using the phrase "How likely is it that. . . ?" Without this modeling many of the questions they developed could be answered with a simple yes or no and not provide parents with the opportunity for decision making. The parents were asked to mark their answers on a Line of Possibility.

The following day children shared with the rest of the class the results from questioning their parents. Most students were able to predict the answers their parents gave; however, many were surprised at some responses.

> MS. ALLEN: Last night you had to collect some data at home. You had to record the data in a different way than we normally record data. You used a Line of Possibility. How did you begin the questions that you asked your parents?
>
> LINDA FAY: I said, "How likely is it?"
>
> MS. ALLEN: How did you explain the homework to your parents?

The children continued by connecting the class work to the homework assignment by recalling how they explained to their parents how to record data on the Line of Possibility. The students next looked at the data collected from their parents and made inferences about why their parents answered the way they did.

> MS. ALLEN: Would someone please share a question you wrote, and tell us how your parent answered it?
>
> LINDA FAY: I asked my mom, "How likely is it that I can baby-sit my neighbor's little children?" She told me fifty-fifty or equally likely.
>
> MS. ALLEN: What do you think she meant by her answer?
>
> LINDA FAY: I think she meant that it was likely that I could baby-sit because she knows I'm good with little kids and that I would take care of them. But it is unlikely because she's afraid that I might not know what to do in case of an emergency.
>
> MS. ALLEN: You've just made an inference, Linda Fay. You've taken the data that you have collected, thought about it, and then you came up with a logical reason why your mother answered the question the way she did.
>
> WESLEY: I asked my mom, "How likely is it that there will be people working on my house when I go home from school?" She said, "Seventy-five percent

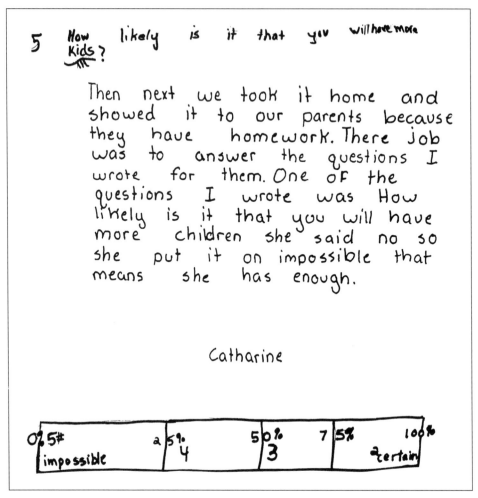

5 How likely is it that you will have more Kids?

Then next we took it home and showed it to our parents because they have homework. There job was to answer the questions I wrote for them. One of the questions I wrote was How likely is it that you will have more children she said no so she put it on impossible that means she has enough.

Catharine

02 5#   a 5%   50%   7 5%   100%
impossible   4   3   certain

FIGURE 3–3   *Catharine's work on the Line of Possibility*

likely because since our house was flooded this spring, there is usually some-one there every day to fix something."

After analyzing and sharing their data, the children spent some time reflecting on the mathematics, and wrote about what they understood about the task. Many times we list questions on the board that students can use to help them begin their reflections. Sometimes the questions are optional, but sometimes we ask the students to use one or more of the questions as points of reflection. The following represent the questions suggested that day:

- What did you learn from your data?
- Choose one question from your survey. Did you predict it would be answered the way your parent responded?
- How does the Line of Possibility work?

Eight-year-old Korine was able to explain very simply what she understood about the Line of Possibility and its connection to data collecting (see Figure 3–2).

Eight-year-old Catharine was also able to express her understanding of the Line of Possibility, but her connection was made to the real world. Her mother emphatically told her "No more children!" (see Figure 3–3).

Opportunities to make connections across the curriculum and across the children's real-life experiences will help them form an integrated network of mathematical ideas and encourage them to see the usefulness of mathematics. It is essential that children recognize relationships among mathematical concepts, use mathematics in all content areas, and see and use mathematics in their everyday living.

Other books that can be used to think about certain and impossible are *Masai and I* by Virginia Kroll and *Anna Banana and Me* by Lenore Blegvad.

Through the use of quilts, coins, and number lines, we found that the hands-on, cooperative tasks that connect mathematics to both girls and stories create exciting opportunities to develop concepts. By exploring and looking at ways to raise our own awareness about including a variety of role models, we became more effective with all children in the class. Every child became an enthusiastic participant.

Works Cited

BELENKY, MARY, BLYTHE CLINCHY, NANCY GOLDBERGER, and JILL TARULE. 1986. *Women's Ways of Knowing: The Development of Self, Voice, and Mind.* New York: Basic Books.

CAMPBELL, PATRICIA. 1995. "Redefining the 'girl problem in mathematics'." In *New Directions for Equity in Mathematics Education*, edited by Walter G. Secada, Elizabeth Fennema, and Lisa Byrd Adajian, 225–241. New York: Cambridge University Press.

FENNEMA, ELIZABETH, and JULIA SHERMAN. 1978. "Sex-Related Differences in Mathematics Achievement, Spatial Visualization, and Sociocultural Factors." *American Educational Research Journal* 14 (1): 51–71.

LEDER, GILAH. 1990. "Gender Differences in Mathematics: An Overview." In *Mathematics and Gender*, edited by Elizabeth Fennema and Gilah Leder, 128–148. New York: Teachers College Press.

WILL, JERRIE ANN, PATRICIA SELF, and NANCY DATAN. 1976. "Maternal Behavior and Perceived Sex of Infant." *American Journal of Orthopsychiatry* 46 (1): 135–39.

Children's Literature

BLEGVAD, LENORE. 1985. *Anna Banana and Me.* New York: Macmillian Publishing Company.

BURNINGHAM, JOHN. 1977. *Come Away from the Water, Shirley.* New York: HarperCollins.

KROLL, VIRGINIA. 1992. *Masai and I*. New York: Four Winds Press.

MATHIS, SHARON BELL. 1975. *The Hundred Penny Box*. New York: Puffin Books.

McCULLY, EMILY ARNOLD. 1992. *Mirette on the Highwire*. New York: Putnam Publishing Group.

———. 1997. *Starring Mirette and Bellini*. New York: Putnam & Grosset Group.

MILLS, LAUREN. 1993. *The Rag Coat*. Boston: Little, Brown.

PAUL, ANN WHITFORD. 1992. *Eight Hands Round: A Patchwork Alphabet*. New York: Harper Collins.

———. 1996. *The Seasons Sewn*. Orlando, FL: Harcourt Brace & Company.

SALLER, CAROL. 1991. *The Bridge Dancers*. Minneapolis, MN: Carolrhoda Books.

Books on Quilting

COBB, MARY. 1995. *The Quilt Block History of Pioneer Days*. Brookfield, CT: Millbrook Press.

COERR, ELEANOR. 1986. *The Josefina Story Quilt*. New York: Harper Trophy Books.

FLOURNOY, VALERIE. 1985. *The Patchwork Quilt*. New York: Dial Books for Young Readers.

———. 1995. *Tanya's Reunion*. New York: Dial Books for Young Readers.

HOPKINSON, DEBORAH. 1993. *Sweet Clara and the Freedom Quilt*. New York: Alfred A. Knopf.

HOWARD, ELLEN. 1996. *The Log Cabin Quilt*. New York: Holiday House.

JONAS, ANN. 1994. *The Quilt*. New York: Puffin Books.

KINSEY-WARNOCK, NATALIE. 1989. *The Canada Geese Quilt*. New York: Cobblehill Books/Dutton.

POLACCO, PATRICIA. 1998. *The Keeping Quilt*. New York: Simon & Schuster Books for Young Readers.

RINGGOLD, FAITH. 1991. *Tar Beach*. New York: Crown Publishers.

SMUCKER, BARBARA. 1995. *Selina and the Bear Claw Quilt*. New York: Crown Publisher.

STEVENS, KATHLEEN. 1994. *Aunt Skilly and the Stranger*. New York: Ticknor & Fields Books for Young Readers.

WILLING, KAREN BATES, and JULIE BATES DOCK. 1994. *Quilting Now and Then*. Ashland, OR: Now & Then Publications.

ZAGWYN, DEBORAH TURNEY. 1990. *The Pumpkin Blanket*. Berkeley, CA: Celestial Arts.

4

Building Critical Friends

Males tend to prefer competitive learning activities while females prefer cooperative learning situations (Isaacson 1990). Yet, as is often pointed out, traditional components of mathematics instruction foster competitive types of behavior (Damarin 1990). Damarin categorizes these features as competition with the computer, with the clock, or with one another. She suggests that reducing the focus on these elements can result in the lessening of the "distancing" females often express regarding mathematical tasks.

In such competitive environments females often defer to others in the name of protecting and safeguarding "relationships" (Miller 1991). Many girls would rather withdraw from an activity than beat a friend.

Connected Environments

A teaching and learning environment grounded on interactions that are "collaborative, cooperative, and interactive" are key linkages to more successful female student performance (Miller 1987, 52). As girls learn more in group situations they have been shown to learn more about themselves. The "inner sense of connection to others" is seen as a "central organizing feature of women's development" (Miller 1991, 11). Newman and Newman (1979) describe female adolescents as frequently trying on a group identity for size as they attempt to determine who they are, hence the power of working with a diverse group of students. Surrey (1991) states that for girls and women "the primary experience of self is relational, that is, the self is organized and developed in the context of important relationships" (52). Girls, who are connected learners, gain knowledge by being engaged in the experiences of others.

Clearly, girls can face more demanding work with more successful outcomes when they are not working in isolation. Interactions with their group and the teacher help them work through problems in a more self-motivated model of instruction. When teachers ask questions that prompt discussion, this model encourages the group conversation needed to help females think through the process. Teachers are likely to take the role of the facilitator at this stage by trying to keep the students' focus on the subject matter, throwing out some thinking questions, rerouting or redirecting if necessary, and in general keeping the thinking coming from the students—not the teacher. Providing a balance of structure and freedom develops risk taking in incremental levels.

Students who leave school as good test-takers find that test-taking ability is not necessarily a skill that will help them be successful on the job; interacting successfully with others will. Since boys often need to learn interaction models other than competitive ones, collaborative learning arrangements are an advantage for all students.

Simply placing students in groups of four is not the cooperative learning of which we speak. Individuals within such a group might be just as competitive as in any other configuration. In fact, as the interactions between and among students move away from the teacher's full viewing range, the teacher must become a more vigilant observer and more skilled in his or her interventions. The nature of the learning in these groups is critical. Teachers should try to avoid the commonplace use of all-boy and all-girl groupings, which continually pit girls against boys.

Effective group learning process is taught, not automatically encountered when students are placed on teams. In the beginning of the year we review the way students might work, and we have found debriefing at the conclusion of the task is important. It is in those conversations that the class shares what was learned on several important levels: mathematics, teamwork, and ways they can be more successful in the future. We know that students who are actively engaged in meaningful tasks, who try to figure out information on their own, who work hand in hand with others, who talk in groups about their questions and solutions bring away more solid and significant learning than children who routinely memorize mathematical procedures. This group learning process, whether labeled networking or cooperative learning, is an essential learning strategy for students.

Cooperative learning must include a self-assessing process where students raise their learning to self-critical levels. In groups, students should probe and critically evaluate their own thinking. A cooperative model where students ask questions of each other such as "Are we sticking to the question?" or "Do we need to consider another perspective or point of view?" helps them reflect on the learning experience. To ensure everyone is an active learner, in advance of putting students in groups, we state that everyone should be ready to be called on to share the group's work. This advanced warning gets everyone invested in helping one another to keep on track using their best thinking while ensuring concepts are understood by all. We expect the members of the group to be responsible for one another's learning. Often as part of assessing students' knowledge we ask them to detail what they have learned but we add "Describe the classmate they learned the most from and why." This formal attention signals to the working groups the value of helping each other.

The benefits of student networking are immense. Children are able to explain their mathematical ideas to others, listen to strategies presented by their peers, ask questions of others, and agree and disagree on solutions to problems. This small group setting allows students, particularly girls, to practice their thinking in a smaller group before presenting those ideas to the entire class. We also find that pulling ourselves out of the conversational equation encourages students to ask more questions, to admit confusion and errors, and to build camaraderie and group spirit. This "teacher-free" time for thinking and sharing requires that students take additional leadership, bring their own meaning and expertise to the concepts and skills of mathematics, and actually become more independent learners.

When engaged in group work, we immediately know if the prompt is going to succeed. The level of conversation between members increases rapidly if there is a great deal of frustration or if roadblocks are identified. Often, we use this signal as an opportunity to regroup as a full class for some more explicit strategy talk. These interchanges occasionally become a mini seminar on a previously taught skill or one group's sharing questions that have arisen with the whole group. In some cases, a tool might be modeled or we give students a "what if . . ." situation to scaffold a connection to another problem that is more familiar.

As we mentioned before, these team problems are rarely completed in a single class session. We encourage students to reflect with their group members and extend their team to other people including parents, siblings, and friends. This time away from the immediate task gives them perspective and the chance to think. The group also knows that they will need to construct a way to share their findings, to communicate in writing the process they went through to solve the problem and justify their use of strategies. The focus is not on having the group find the one right answer, but on finding many ways that the problem could be solved.

Most of the work we suggest throughout this book includes students working in cooperative settings. The literature and lessons we highlight in this chapter exemplify not only a team approach but also the extension of the cooperation and connections to others that is so successful with female learners.

Not Your Average . . .

Swamp Angel, a Caldecott honor award winning book by Anne Isaacs, spins a Tennessee folk tale of Angelica Longrider. Angelica was "scarcely taller than her mother at birth, and although she was given an ax in the cradle she was already two before she built her first log cabin." Angelica was a very special young woman. Her nickname Swamp Angel came after she rescued a wagon train out of a marsh at the age of twelve.

When the call goes out across the land for someone to help rid the territory of a huge bear known as Thundering Tarnation who was stealing the townspeople's food, Angelica is ready to try. After unsuccessful attempts by male competitors, Angelica rises to the challenge. The battle of strength and will lasts for days and nights, but Angelica persists and succeeds and then treats all of Tennessee and Kentucky to the bear feast.

The tall tale of Angelica led to interesting student discussions of fantasy, reality, and fiction writing. Students even touched on the issue of animal rights when Angelica battled the bear, pointing out that "the bear was just doing what was natural. If we saw some food just sitting there we would want to take it too." The outrageous situations created in this tale, however, helped them see the exaggerations as part of the humor.

Students found that thinking about what Angelica was able to do at a given age stirred their imagination. Thinking about what could be done if a person was two hundred feet tall encouraged everyone to fantasize. One child observed, "She would be the first one to know if it was going to rain, because she would feel it first." Another child saw a relationship between a recent investigation of the Olympic Torch Relay and Swamp Angel's size when she suggested that "if she were running in the relay she would need to take only one step to go one kilometer."

Mathematical connections came about from the fact that Angelica was not like everyone else in size, strength, and skill. Discussions about the story led to the mathematical opportunity to work on measures of central tendency, as students gathered data about themselves and made comparisons. The *Swamp Angel* prompt was introduced, and it encouraged students to imagine what being above average in size, strength, and skill would be like. Then they were asked to focus on what is average in their lives. They were asked to conduct mathematical research to find out about what is "average." This investigation allowed the students to direct an exploration of what they would like to learn about other children their own age.

Students first agreed that they wanted to collect numerical data. Then they brainstormed questions, discussed the possibilities, and came to consensus on what information they wanted to know. They decided to survey students in their age range, nine- to eleven-year-olds, and gather information on height, weight, shoe size, and hours of TV watched per day. They also were persistent about knowing whether most children were left- or right-handed. These data did not fit the criterion of numerical responses and later presented a challenge when students used spreadsheets. They were each responsible for collecting data on the five questions from twenty individuals within the designated age range. The students worked independently to gather their data and to compile and average the information.

Students in the class were previously introduced to spreadsheets and decided that they wanted to put their information from their survey in this format. With help from our technological support team, they designed a spreadsheet for use in organizing and analyzing the data (see Figure 4–1). This included the decision to code data for right and left hands into ones and zeros. The spreadsheet activity helped them recheck their data and gave students more practice in developing appropriate formulas to calculate totals and the mean. One student explained in her reflections, "We had to put formulas in the computer to get the average, the formula for weight, for

Swamp Angel Random Survey

	A	B	C	D	E	F
1	**NAME**	**HEIGHT**	**WEIGHT**	**SHOE SIZE**	**HRS. TV**	**R/L**
2	Brad j.	62	110	10.5	2	1
3	Danny	48	55	2.5	2.5	1
4	Leah	56	65	4	5	1
5	Brandy	60	82	7.5	8	1
6	Christy	58	49	6.2	4	1
7	Kenya	53	84	6.2	4	1
8	Tye	56	84	6.2	4	1
9	Jessica	66	63	5.2	4	1
10	Irania	73	100	6	1	1
11	Tyler	57	95	8	6	1
12	Brandon	4.8	65	5.2	1	1
13	Jenny	56	70	4	2.2	1
14	Victor	56	54	3	2.2	1
15	Ben B.	59	80	7	2	0
16	Jonathen	5	80	7	3	1
17	Ariel f.	4	70	5.2	2.2	1
18	Heather	5.3	95	4	2	1
19	mike B.	5.8	64	7	5	1
20	Nicole I.	4.8	65	3	5	1
21	Travis	4.8	74	7	3	0
22	**AVERAGE**	39.725	75.2	5.735	3.405	
23					right	18
24					left	2

FIGURE 4-1   *Ashley's Swamp Angel spreadsheet*

example, =avg(C2..C21)." She also added that the computer calculated the average faster and more accurately. This reorganization of information also reinforced the NCTM Standard relating to students' constructing, reading, and interpreting displays of data.

Some students then asked what the response might be of students in other parts of the country. With the help of e-mail through friends at the university and colleagues at neighboring school districts, the questions were sent to other parts of the country and Canada with the resulting information electronically returned to the class. These data were also transferred to spreadsheets, and students compared and contrasted the averages in height, weight, shoe size, hours of TV watched, and the totals of how many students were right- or left-handed. Several mathematical activities emerged as a result of the e-mail information. The measurements sent from other schools did not always come in inches, and some were in decimal form while others used fractions. This was a teachable moment. The students had to investigate how to convert feet to inches, and in some cases, centimeters to inches. They also had an opportunity to place their class's numerical data side by side with a class from another city and write mathematical conjectures about the comparisons. A child wrote, "The tallest and shortest came from the other class [New York] data." In looking at other comparisons a student wrote, "For example our average height was 56.35 [inches] and theirs was 59 so that proves that they were taller than us. The average shoe size was 5.8 but the other class average was 6.1, so that meant they also had bigger feet." Another child summarized her data in the following way: "We found out the average fourth grader is right-handed, watches 3 hours of TV a day, has a shoe size of about 5, weighs 76.75 pounds and their height is 56 inches."

Some students decided to actually use the data to create a "real" version of AverageKid. Using a roll of brown paper they took the average measurements already collected to help them form the prototypical student. They started by marking off the height and then tried to find someone the exact weight of 76.75 pounds. Then they realized that although the person was the correct weight they were smaller in height. When the person lay down on the paper the group realized that the proportion would not be accurate. When they found a closer match in height and weight to the statistics, they traced the body estimating a little more weight in some places. The shoe size was added when they again found a child with an exact match. To report the data on which hand is most often used, a replica of a pencil was glued to AverageKid's right hand. Some children wanted to add other data, so they found the average pulse rate in the class and added that number to a heart-shaped outline on AverageKid's chest. Of course it was interesting to the students that, although this was the average child, none of them actually had all of the average characteristics. The concrete version of the data helped some children see connections that they had not made before.

The students wrote reflectively about what they found about students in their corner of the world from interpreting their survey data. This activity linked well with the NCTM Standard of Communication that suggests that students should realize that representing, discussing, reading, writing, and listening to mathematics are vital parts of their lives.

Since the children are in the multiage classes for more than one year, this activity began at the end of one school year and awaited the children at the beginning of the next. Throughout the investigation and data collection, the teacher kept asking the students about the people who would need to know this information. How could we share our findings with the real world? Who would be interested in shoe sizes, height, weight, TV watching, and handedness of children in different parts of the continent? Students considered whether this information might be valuable in marketing products to people their age. The consensus came down to several groups that might use the findings: shoe companies, clothing companies, and manufacturers of scissors. Although letters were written to these groups regarding the possible implications of the survey results, as we write the class was still waiting for a response.

Angelica Longrider was a risk taker. Her example led the class on a continentwide search for data on how the students compared with other nine-, ten-, and eleven-year-olds. Her "hardy personality" gave us an avenue to grow more knowledgeable about our world and ourselves.

Another book that can be used with this lesson is *Sally Ann Thunder Ann Whirlwind Crockett*, a tall tale retold by Steven Kellogg.

Creative Cartography

The book *Sweet Clara and the Freedom Quilt* by Deborah Hopkinson is a perfect companion to a unit of study about the Civil War. Since students had already investigated the life of the risk taker Harriet Tubman, including her courageous involvement with the Underground Railroad, in the book *Wanted Dead or Alive: The True Story of Harriet Tubman*, they already had a strong background for the story.

Clara worked as a seamstress on a plantation in the South. When she hears about people's dream for a lasting set of directions to help slaves reach the safety of the north, she connects the need to her skill with a needle and thread. She begins to sew together a fabric map that she refers to as the freedom quilt. It is this quilt that can lead people to a new home. After we read Clara's story the students discussed the design of her quilt and how it played a role in her own escape.

The activity that followed was developed as a way to assess students' retention of the concepts of area and perimeter. Students were placed in groups and were given table-sized pieces of one-inch-square grid paper and the prompt for the quilt. They were asked to create a complete design for an imagined escape, which could include either a map of our school grounds or the local neighborhood (see Figure 4–2). Once the students started the activity, the classroom was buzzing and students were plotting and planning the design of their quilt to match the features of their chosen locale. Because we gave broad parameters in the size of their project, students spent a good deal of time discussing the best fit and scale within the limitations of the grid paper.

Most students used the maximum space provided and added color to make the maps easier to interpret. Then they found the area and perimeter for the obstacles on their quilt maps. The students recorded these measurements on a chart and wrote about the strategies used to calculate this information. Many groups used a labor-intensive counting strategy by which they counted the full grid squares inside the shape for area and the edges of the grid squares making up the figures for perimeter. Others used a mix of strategies where they calculated a large area and subtracted out

Sweet Clara and The Freedom Quilt
By Deborah Hopkinson

Performance Event
       * Design a quilt like map*

Criteria:
1. Quilt/map must fill the greater part of the grid paper you have been given.

2. Your quilt/map must show a minimum of five places that could include buildings, trees, railroad tracks, etc.

3. All members of the group should contribute to the product.

4. Area and perimeter of the quilt/map should be recorded on the final product.

WRITING ABOUT YOUR QUILT/ MAP

1. Describe your quilt/map. Could someone match your quilt/map with your description?

2. What is the area of the largest place/object on your quilt/map? How did you find the area?

3. What is the perimeter of the smallest place/object on your quilt/map? How did you find the perimeter?

4. Explain your choice of tools in finding the area and perimeter. What second strategy and tools could you have used to find area and perimeter?

5. Assess yourself as a member of this group. How did you contribute to the work? Explain how your group worked cooperatively.

FIGURE 4–2   Sweet Clara *performance event prompt*

smaller portions. The irregular shapes with curved edges were the most challenging. The writing provided a clear picture of which students were able to make connections between previous instruction and the new task.

Students also wrote an individual description of the map. The narrative was to be so descriptive that reading their piece would enable anyone to locate their group's project. This kind of detail required a command of mathematical detail and terminology.

As with many of our collaborative projects, for closure we focused the discussion of each member's contribution and how the group worked together to help everyone understand the process and outcome. It was enlightening to hear how the division of labor played out in the different groups. Without these debriefing sessions students can miss out on the critical development of "people skills." Also, students quickly recognize the accountability for all members of the group. The objective is to have them examine their role in group efforts and to continue to grow as a problem solver and team player.

Clara's quilt provided a secret way to furnish a diagram to people long ago who were looking for a secure passageway to the north. Today, quilts are also able to communicate. In our exploration of quilted maps students located an Internet site that included a quilt contest with a theme of "If Quilts Could Talk." The quilts are listed by the best in each state, grand prize winners, and nine awards recognizing the work of children. Each quilt includes the maker's story and in some cases the actual dimensions of the finished product. If you click on the image of the quilt a screen-sized version will appear. The site can be reached at: "http://www.landsend.com/spawn. cgi?NODELIQW0896&GRAPHIC&NODEZERO0795_". The students were touched by many of the stories and enjoyed seeing our state champion and those from states where students had extended family. They used measuring tools to demonstrate the size of the winning projects on the classroom floor, which helped in calculating the area and the perimeter of each.

At the same time, another quilt that told a story was in the news. The AIDS quilt acts as a record of the lives that were lost to this disease. Ten years ago the quilt had 1,920 patches and covered an area about the size of a city block. Today the quilt weighs forty-two tons, contains one mile of fabric, is composed of almost 40,000 patches, and can cover the entire Washington, DC, mall, from the Capitol building to the Washington Monument. Even so, it is a remembrance of only a fraction of the people who have died. As we discussed the quilt with the class, we found the mathematics and the message were both powerful. A legacy quilt might be an appropriate gift for the graduating elementary school class to make for the school. The mathematics they would use to complete such a storytelling quilt could be a rich remembrance of their contributions to the school.

Many quilt projects tie into local history; neighborhood groups often create quilts that have a story. By linking the classroom mathematics to the community, much can be gained.

Both Sides Now

The Bedspread, by Sylvia Fair, is a sweet story of two elderly sisters, Maud and Amelia. They live on either end of a long, long bed in an old, old house. The sisters are creative and cooperative problem solvers. Being quite bored with their plain white bedspread, they decide jointly to add some handiwork that will depict a view of their childhood home.

From each end of the bed, the sisters alternate in calling out instructions to each other so that their design will contain as many stitches as possible and be symmetrical. Maud is the precise artist who uses embroidery as her form of needlework, while Amelia, who has forgotten the intricate stitches, uses appliqué as her medium. The resulting bedspread design, while not truly symmetrical, is a breathtaking piece of artwork worthy of displaying in the local museum.

Having worked with symmetry throughout the year, we decided to give students a task that would test several areas of understanding. After reading *The Bedspread* for a second time, the students searched for the math wisdom. Students talked about the symmetrical design of the houses on the bedspread. They were able to point out the parts of the design that were nearly symmetrical and the parts that were very different. Here are some of the students' comments on the symmetry:

MS. ALLEN: Ashleigh, you said that the bedspread was symmetrical. Explain your thinking.

ASHLEIGH: Symmetrical means that something is the same on both sides. Both houses have a garden, the same number of windows, steps, chimneys, and other things that are alike.

LAUREN: But it has to be a mirror image, too. It can't just have the same things. It has to be in the same place on the page as a reflection.

MS. ALLEN: How could you prove that the sisters' designs are symmetrical?

LAUREN: You could hold a mirror on one side and see if you see the same thing on the other side when you lift the mirror.

COOPER: On the bedspread you won't see exactly the same thing because they used different sewing to make their houses.

BRITTANY: Amelia had children climbing up the house but Maud didn't.

MS. ALLEN: So, in some ways the bedspread was nearly symmetrical, but in some ways the symmetry was thrown off. Today you will begin an activity that blends mathematics and art. This will allow us to see how well you work together, how well you can communicate directions to a partner, and how well you understand symmetry.

Students were asked to work with a partner to create their own bedspread banner. Like the sisters, the partners would sit on the opposite sides of the paper and take turns being responsible for giving directions for part of the house. The directions needed to be given so that the designs were symmetrical. Each house was to have at least the house frame, a door, steps, a railing, a garden, and windows. The partners could then add any other details that they wanted to include. Each duo was given a twenty-four-inch-by-thirty-six-inch sheet of white drawing paper, the prompt, and a cardboard divider so that the children could follow the directions without looking at each other's work.

As a combined mathematics and art project the students were given a specific rubric that would remind them of what would be included in a high quality piece of work. The banners would have multiple examples of symmetry, use measurement, demonstrate spatial sense, and include explanations for how they knew they met these criteria.

As students began their work, they were reminded to identify a way to communicate what they wanted drawn and where. We observed and recorded how different partners approached the task. Some students immediately folded the paper in half to replicate the "safety pin line" down the center of the sisters' bedspread. Others used a meter stick, measured the halfway point, marked, and drew a line. A small group of students did not stop long enough to find the center of the paper, but instead dove straight into the task. It was interesting, however, to contrast the partners who began the task without having any preliminary conversations with those who discussed their strategies before jumping into the work. Some teams practiced using vocabulary that would help each member know exactly where to place a piece of the house.

> DESIREE: If I say that my window is on my right, then what will you do?
> NATALIE: Then I would put it on my right. But if we both hold up our right hands they're on opposite sides.
> GRETCHEN: We'd have to say, "My window is on my left, so put your window on the right." That way the windows will be mirror images.
> NINA: Jeremy is getting me confused. How do I know where to put the door exactly? Can we use rulers to measure and tell them the measurement or is that cheating?
> KEVIN: That's not cheating. You just can't show them where to put the ruler. You have to tell them exact directions and measurements.

The conversations and collaboration continued, and we were able to take anecdotal notes on how the partnerships were progressing. Some students had little patience with each other, while others were more successful in communicating their wishes. This is to be expected as children in a multiage classroom are at very different levels of understanding.

After the main components of the project were completed, the children were able to move the cardboard dividers to see how their directions were working. Then they decided if they wanted to color their designs exactly alike or to work as Maud and Amelia did and make their own choices. Some partners continued to keep the cardboard dividers up and instructed their teammates as to how to add details to the drawing.

After two days of working on the bedspread banner, the children gathered to talk about the last part of their task. Together each partnership was asked to reflect on and discuss several questions and then to come back to share some of those thoughts with the whole class before they wrote independently in their journals.

Ms. ALLEN: Which directions were most helpful in making your house?

MEGAN: I liked it when Sean gave me directions to measure up six inches from the bottom and then measure three inches across and then draw a one-inch square. I could follow that kind the best because I could use a ruler.

HEATHER: The most helpful thing was when Evan said to put the tree on my right because he put it on his left.

Ms. ALLEN: Which directions did you find most confusing and why?

LAUREN: The really confusing ones were the ones for the railing and the steps. He said to go down from the steps and then crisscross, but I didn't understand what he really meant. We needed better math vocabulary words to describe what we were doing.

WESLEY: I gave a confusing direction to my partner. On the trees I meant to say the width of the tree was three centimeters, but by accident I said three inches. So, the tree was in the right place it was just way too big.

Ms. ALLEN: How did you plan together to make sure your directions would give you a drawing that would be symmetrical?

MEGAN: We had to practice telling that something was on my right and your left. We really had to use exact directions. Then we practiced and folded the picture in half to see if it would be symmetrical. It was a little off.

LINDA FAY: We also repeated the directions to make sure because it was really hard.

Ms. ALLEN: If you were able to try this project again, what changes would you make in giving directions or in following directions?

JAMESON: I would use the ruler to give more exact directions. You really need to have a good partner and not argue with them.

SARAH: I would listen very carefully to the math vocabulary words. You really have to think about what you are saying before you do it. I think that you really have to work together at the beginning to make it come out right.

CATHARINE: You really have to know what symmetry is. It's not as easy as it looks.

Working as partners and in small groups of three and four definitely demands that students work well together. Teachers cannot assume that cooperative interactions come naturally with all students. Cooperative work should be taught so that students will understand expectations and practice those skills needed for working together.

Walk the Mathtalk

Counting on Jenny, by Helena Clare Pittman, is a lively story of an observant young girl. The title strongly suggests a mathematical connection, and Jenny definitely is busy counting. As she heads to school each day, she uses what could be a routine bus excursion to enumerate much of what she sees. As we read the story to the class, we asked the students to keep a record of the items she counted. Even the best listeners were challenged as they attempted to keep track of all the things she added and subtracted. Jenny's love of numbers and the pleasure she gained from seeing the mathematics around her gave us the idea to develop a Math-Walk. The walk would incorporate all the mathematics concepts we studied such as number and computation, geometry and measurement, probability and statistics, and algebraic ideas.

> Ms. BROWN: What do you think a Math-Walk is?
> BEN: Is it like the walking tour of our school's tree museum, but instead you walk around and learn about math?
> Ms. BROWN: Good thinking. What kind of connections can we make with Jenny's counting experience and what we might do?
> STEPHANIE: She found some of the math concepts on her bus ride. She used number computation too.
> Ms. BROWN: We might want to look for ways we see math concepts around our school. We need to make sure that we have a nice blend of mathematical ideas in our walk so that people taking our Math-Walking tour will learn the many different ways we find mathematics around us.

To give students a model, we reviewed with the class a Math-Walk created by a middle school team. Although the mathematics was more complex, we wanted students to see the variety of questions and the focus on mathematical ideas. Students picked up on the words *symmetry*, *axis*, and *cylinder* in the questions from the model. We instructed the groups to use their "mathematical-logical intelligence" as they walked around collecting data to write problems. We told them that they should remember to refer to objects that couldn't be moved so the Math-Walk could be a lasting mathematical tour. The students quickly set out in search of ideas.

After the initial collection of data, students returned and began writing thoughts on chart paper. We used these ideas to type up a first draft, and made sure that we honored their wording. The next day students examined the questions, began peer-revising sessions, and then added more detail to the Math-Walk. The first draft consisted of many computational questions, and each group seemed to focus on the school's fire extinguishers. Questions at that point included: What is the shape of a fire extinguisher? How tall is a fire extinguisher? What is the width of a fire extinguisher?

The class revisited the example of the Math-Walk from the middle school with an eye for the range of mathematics that could be incorporated. Then students recognized that there were whole topics of mathematics that they had neglected. They also began asking if some questions could only be answered by using measuring tools and calculators. Michael suggested that the class add a border of centimeters on one margin and inches across the bottom of the paper, so that the actual Math-Walk document could be a tool for estimating and measuring. During the first revision session, each group focused on making the directions clearer and less confusing. We took their ideas and edits and returned with the second edition. On this day they went out to test their questions and to find answers.

When the groups returned, we conferenced with each table separately to note their discoveries and evaluate their progress. We saw more changes in their questions, as they moved from thinking about "how many" toward higher level or more open-ended inquiries. For example, one group wanted the Math-Walk participant to find the area of the floor in the cove (the cul-de-sac between four clustered classrooms). In the revision process, some felt specific calculations of area might be too time-consuming, so they rephrased it to read, "Estimate the area of the floor in the cove, and tell what strategy you used." Another group initially wanted the person going on the Math-Walk to count the water fountains in the hall. After peer discussions, they broadened it to estimating and then keeping track of how many water fountains could be found. Instead of asking the Math-Walkers to merely count the lockers, they moved to requesting the Math-Walk participants to identify and draw geometric patterns they found on the lockers.

The third day marked our third revision and the actual field testing of our product. This practice run would test our own knowledge as well. Upon completion, students concluded that they had created a challenging Math-Walk. The questions the students designed for the Math-Walk ranged from simple counting and computation to finding geometric shapes, ratios, fractions, and measurements.

> "Look at the murals on the cafeteria walls. What is the ratio of the number of animals to the number of hooves? What is the ratio of the number of eyeballs to the number of living beings?"
> "What geometric shapes do you see in the lockers?"
> "Go up one flight of stairs. How many stairs did you climb? What would half of that number equal?"

Now they were anxious to test the walk with their math buddies, young partners they mentor from a multiage primary class.

The students were paired with their math buddies and set out to try a portion of the Math-Walk. Many were particularly interested in field testing the part of the walk that they created so they were sure to steer their buddies in that direction. Here are some students' comments after they returned to the classroom:

JOSEPH: The question we wrote about finding the shape on the door and how many of that shape could you find in the building was impossible. There are so many rectangles. The lockers, the cinder blocks, and a million other things.

MS. BROWN: How could we change that question to make it more manageable? Think about that for a while.

JILL: I was really surprised that there were only thirty-four water fountains in our school. I had never stopped to think about that before.

KELLY: The question that asked you to find the sum of six three-digit numbers was too hard for the buddies.

MS. BROWN: What would you change?

KELLY: I think they only should have three or four numbers to add.

DEREK: On the question that asked you to use a strategy to predict the flagpole height—my math buddy didn't know any strategies for measuring height.

MYKEL: My partner was too short, so we had to boost him up to measure the fish tank in the office.

LIBBY: I have an idea that would help fix the question that Joseph was concerned about. How about just asking how many doorways and looking for that number. That would be very basic math though.

MATT: The measuring tool on the side of the paper was not real easy for some of the younger students to use.

JAMIE: I think we should keep this one for adults and older students, but I think we may want to make a "Math-Walk Junior." We might need to make it easier to read. For example, instead of using the word ratio we would say count and compare the number of chairs to the number of tables.

JILL: I think if we make a primary version, we should use more pictures and a simpler vocabulary.

MS. BROWN: How have you grown mathematically from designing this Math-Walk?

JOSIE: I really understand ratio better.

JAMIE: I felt really proud, that I wrote some of these questions, and that made it easier for me to explain to my math buddy. Why not help our math buddies create their own walk with the math they can do?

From observing students write and refine mathematical problems, we collected strong evidence of their growth in mathematical understanding and their ability to identify mathematics concepts. The initial draft was riddled with many mathematical holes, and we wanted to see if teams could analyze the problems and come to consensus on revisions. We did discover that trying to revise with twenty-eight students was not the optimal situation. When we engaged the large group in another problem-solving activity so we could conference with small groups, we were able to see rapid improvement. In the large group, students only felt responsible for their own questions and only revised accordingly. When working in the collaborative groups, students took more ownership of the project and became more motivated to reach a quality product.

We saw their mathematical communication skills grow in using mathematical terminology in real-world applications. This was a cooperative effort where group members prized a student's logical reasoning skills. We know the mathematical leaders tried to make all the decisions, but the groups continued to use consensus on finalizing questions.

Many people suggest that a true group activity is one in which no single group member could complete the project as well without the help of the team. This was truly the case in this lesson. The combined effort paid off with a thought-provoking Math-Walk that can be used by any visitor to our school.

By developing networks of critical friends, students can broaden their thinking and communication skills. The networks we tried included pairs, threesomes, small groups, and the whole class as they linked to other students in other states and countries, teachers, parents, and community members. The problem-solving activities we tried ranged from independently gathering data about the "average kid," designing a quilt map with a small group, creating a symmetrical bedspread with a partner, to developing a Math-Walk with a team of classmates. Through this network of students working collaboratively they were able to expand, analyze, and evaluate their problem-solving ability.

Works Cited

DAMARIN, SUZANNE. 1990. "Teaching Mathematics: A Feminist Perspective." In *Teaching and Learning Mathematics in the 1990's*, edited by Thomas Cooney and Christian Hirsch, 144–51. Reston, VA: NCTM.

ISAACSON, ZELDA. 1990. "'They Look at You in Absolute Horror': Women Writing and Talking About Mathematics." In *Gender and Mathematics: An International Perspective*, edited by Leone Burton, 20–28. New York: Cassell Education.

MILLER, JANET. 1987. "Women as Teachers/Researchers: Gaining a Sense of Ourselves." *Teacher Education Quarterly* 14 (2): 52–58.

MILLER, JEAN B. 1991. "The Development of Women's Sense of Self." In *Women's Growth in Connection: Writings from the Stone Center*, edited by Judith Jordan, Alexandria Kaplan, Jean B. Miller, Irene Stiver, and Janet Surrey, 11–26. New York: Guilford Press.

NEWMAN, BARBARA M., and PHILIP R. NEWMAN. 1979. *Development Through Life*. Chicago: Dorsey Press.

SURREY, JANET L. 1991. "The 'Self-in-Relation': A Theory of Women's Development." In *Women's Growth in Connection: Writings from the Stone Center*, edited by Judith Jordan, Alexandria Kaplan, Jean B. Miller, Irene Stiver, and Janet Surrey, 51–66. New York: Guilford Press.

Children's Literature

FAIR, SYLVIA. 1982. *The Bedspread*. New York: William Morrow and Company.

HOPKINSON, DEBORAH. 1993. *Sweet Clara and the Freedom Quilt*. New York: Alfred A. Knopf.

ISAACS, ANNE. 1994. *Swamp Angel.* New York: Dutton Children's Books.

KELLOGG, STEVEN. 1995. *Sally Ann Thunder Ann Whirlwind Crockett: A Tall Tale.* New York: William Morrow and Company.

McGOVERN, ANN. 1991. *Wanted Dead or Alive: The True Story of Harriet Tubman.* New York: Scholastic.

PITTMAN, HELENA CLARE. 1994. *Counting on Jennie.* Minneapolis, MN: Carolrhoda Books.

RINGGOLD, FAITH. 1993. *Aunt Harriet's Underground Railroad in the Sky.* New York: Crown Publishers.

5

Knowing What Is Known

Mathematics instruction driven by traditional paper-and-pencil assessments is frequently seen as looking for one right answer through one right way to solve the problem. This single-solution and algorithm-centered model has been identified as one that presents a particular obstacle for female students. In an effort to move away from the inequity inherent in the use of conventional standardized or publisher-generated assessment techniques, teachers need to incorporate more authentic and richer options in evaluative models and approaches. Rather than producing a snapshot of behavior on a single day, these assessments create portraits of student growth and achievement. Such alternative models can involve teamwork, performance tasks with manipulative materials, interviews, written reflections, open-ended questions, portfolio prompts, presentations, and self- and peer assessment. These assessments are completely embedded in the instruction, a design that works so well for girls. They capitalize on the use of "girls' ability to synthesize, make connections, and use their practical intelligence" (Pollina 1995, 32).

In the past many of us saved our thoughts on assessment until the end of the unit that we were teaching. As the end loomed near, we would stop and ask, How should I test the students to see if they have learned the mathematics? Much of this testing was looking for breadth, not depth, and did not consider students' learning styles or strengths. Additionally, the "end-of-the-unit-test" was mainly used for giving grades, and the tests that compared our students locally and nationally drove our behaviors from March to May.

In actuality, assessment is still the driving force of our teaching, but instead of teaching for the test, the assessment gauges student learning and informs our instruction. Instruction and assessment are continuous, with the children's knowledge and needs being the guiding force in planning activities and experiences that will move them forward. Now, before we plan teaching activities, we ask ourselves, What do we want students to know and be able to do? and How can we know how well they can do it? During this planning period, we set high expectations for all of our students.

A good performance task should be indistinguishable from a good instructional task. Therefore, the investigations we create do not require special skills that are learned in multiple sessions of performance assessment training. Rather they emerge from what we are already doing in the classroom and reflect what we believe in as educators. Each is based on the tenet of allowing students to demonstrate their ability to connect what they already know to solve novel problem situations in an inquiry-based event. Adding assessment activities that are not fully integrated into the curriculum to the planned instructional activities is not realistic. As a result, we develop tasks that subscribe to a unit perspective, based on big ideas, not small particles of information or isolated skills. In this way the tasks easily mesh with the classroom agenda and actually provide creativity and excitement in our teaching. We are not looking just to measure student performance but also to promote students' mathematical growth and to collect feedback to enhance further instruction.

When we create performance tasks we attempt to include the following features:

- Embedding the situation in a rich and usually real-world context
- Involving a valued curricular goal in mathematics
- Beginning with a problem situation
- Involving individual, partner, or team work
- Incorporating options for material use such as manipulatives or technology
- Requiring communication from students in words, pictures, and numbers
- Requiring that answers be justified and explained in detail
- Creating a culminating event of an oral, written, and/or dramatized product
- Basing the activity on the premise that great minds do not think alike.

Rethinking Report Cards

The shift in assessment styles requires corresponding movement in the kinds of report cards given to parents. If teachers are forced to supply traditional grades, then the benefit of using rubrics is diluted and invalidated. We have heard of teachers taking the rubric grade of "three" on the four-part continuum and translating that into a "B" for report card purposes. This will not work. The report cards we use in much of our state are teacher-written narratives that provide parents with rich and detailed information about their child's performance.

Our teaching team has been using a narrative reporting system for four years. We do not grade or score papers with letter or numerical grades. We use a statewide Learning Profile that includes a list of descriptors and a continuum that details the progress students are likely to follow during their years in elementary school. The information in the descriptors provides teachers with developmental information to record and report individual student growth. The descriptors act as a guide to categorize a student's performance at a particular level or phase.

One of the critical outcomes of using this particular reporting tool is the integration of assessment and instruction while aligning both with content guidelines and standards. The narrative reporting system is designed to give parents, students, and teachers a look at student growth and development in the key components of each academic area. Parents have grown to appreciate the more detailed information. An example of a report card using the Learning Profile descriptors follows:

> Jessica applies computational skills and can add, subtract, multiply, and divide whole numbers up to the ten thousands. She consistently uses estimating strategies and mental mathematics to solve problems. Jessica successfully uses a calculator to problem solve. She can identify place value through 1,000,000. She has progressed with skills in using decimals and fractions in operations. Jessica uses deductive thinking in her problem solving. She consistently selects effective strategies and is beginning to focus on the "why" along with the "how" in her mathematics writing. She can collect and interpret data in a variety of graph formats. Jessica can identify and construct two- and three-dimensional geometric figures. She is competent using both standard and metric units of measure.

Rubrics are data-collecting formats that are not directly related to grades. Because the performance assessment integral to this project focuses on what students know, rubrics must leave latitude by not putting a ceiling on students' responses. Excellence is not achieved by finding a single right answer in a specific way designated by the teacher but by taking the assignment beyond the original expectations. This is not unlike dancers and singers who never feel they quite reach a pinnacle performance; there is always more room for growth. These performers recognize that there is invariably the opportunity to strive for and reach new heights.

You will note that we use two kinds of rubrics, a holistic version and a version specifically tailored to particular problem-solving situations. Many times students are involved in creating the rubric and talking about what they believe would be superior work. By having an open discussion about any given criterion, students are always aware of the characteristics and qualities we are looking for and through the input have a sense of ownership in the product. When the class is working on a major project, parents are given a copy of the rubric as well.

Kidwatching

Teacher observation probably gives one of the truest pictures of what students know and can do. We are attentive to students as they work individually, with a partner, and in group situations. Of particular interest are the group dynamics; here we see who is participating, who the emergent leaders are, who is passively absorbing information, and who insists on pursuing new and different strategies. As students demonstrate evidence of reasoning, strategy use, and conceptual understanding, we are vigilant in observing and recording. Using large sticky labels, we note the child's name and the date, and anecdotal information regarding progress or concerns. At the conclusion of the week these labels are moved to permanent folders for the children who were observed. This record of growth becomes the basis for future planning, report cards, and parent conferences. We find that our own learning is exponential as we first use a "wide-angle lens" to view the whole picture of the classroom, and then a "zoom lens" on each individual.

To begin assessing students using teacher observation, we first choose a skill, strategy, or technique on which we intend to focus. For example, during the assessment work on our *City Green* investigation, each student would be assessed on their choice of tools and strategies and for successfully using them to find the area of a garden plot and dividing it into sections for the neighbors. We like to use a running record style sheet to collect observations for each student in the class.

This matrix enables the teacher to examine the progress of particular children over a week. Although each child is not assessed in this manner every day, in some cases a certain child or group of children may be a focus for a period of days to document learning styles, group dynamics, or strategy use. We maintain a checklist that shows which children have been observed, so that each child will be considered in depth at least once over any two-week period.

Interviewing Learners

The interview is not only a fine individual assessment tool, but it also melds with our vision of connected teaching. Interviews are diagnostic conferences usually held between student and teacher. Normally, we begin with an agenda to discuss particular skills or strategies. Recording what the child knows and can do is the focus. We also establish our reteaching groups through data collected in these sessions.

Frequently the student will come to the table to demonstrate a concept like perimeter or multiplication with available manipulatives. Some sessions may only last a moment or two when we help a student refocus or redirect. Other meetings may involve a more extensive contact where other students may have to consult with peers while the teacher concentrates on this one child or a small group of children. We often wear a visor or "conferencing hat" so that other students know we cannot be disturbed or we sit at a designated "work station." The interview becomes a time for students to ask for more help and direction as well as to spotlight their successes. No matter what the focus, the interview is very helpful in learning more about each individual student in the class.

We recall specifically one young girl, Christy, who was struggling with the concept of division. When she arrived at the table for her interview, Christy lowered her head and would not make eye contact. We asked her to demonstrate a problem that involved sharing thirty-seven cookies with four people, but she was unable to successfully perform the operation and clearly showed her lack of confidence in completing the task. After a short conversation that included commending her on her progress in math, Christy indicated that although she was nervous and unsure she thought she was ready to learn how to divide. We then spent about ten minutes in our interview retracing the underpinnings of the division concept with the corresponding symbolic expressions. We found that during this time together, Christy grew more confident when she was able to think about, act out, and reflect on each problem with another person as an audience. On a continuing basis, we made a point to ask Christy to demonstrate a problem involving a division situation. This practice built her self-assurance and understanding. We began to notice Christy was helping others and giving clues to classmates who had reached division roadblocks.

We kept reminding Christy in subtle and obvious ways that she was a rising mathematician who could meet any challenge. Christy's crowning glory came the day she volunteered to show her solution process to a division problem to the entire class. With this young girl, it took a personal touch and the consistent reinforcing of the positive experience begun in the conference setting to empower her to become an "expert."

Conferencing with Peers

Peer evaluation is a particularly effective approach prior to the completion of a final draft. Students invite a small group to watch their practice presentation, listen to their written work, or examine a model they have constructed. This nonthreatening time for sharing encourages students to sharpen communication skills and fix anything that is unclear.

For peer conferencing to work well, children must see themselves as part of a community of learners. Girls need the security and confidence that the assistance is being offered out of sincere interest. We model the types of praise and suggestions that are important for students who create quality learning products. Humorous role-playing situations suggesting the "dos" and "don'ts" of peer conferencing are helpful in establishing appropriate models of feedback.

Birds of a Feather—Performance Event

Author Kathryn Lasky and illustrator David Catrow blend their talents to create a memorable book about the beginnings of the Massachusetts Audubon Society. *She's Wearing a Dead Bird on Her Head!* helped the students understand the serious impact fashion can have on the environment while giving us the opportunity to assess data collection and analysis skills. In this delightfully written and illustrated book, two women, Minna Hall and Harriet Hemenway, set out to protect the bird population while positioning women to be taken more seriously in society. Minna Hall and Harriet Hemenway problem solving this environmental issue so early in the nineteenth century shows young mathematicians that seemingly impossible tasks can be accomplished when interest and desire are present.

As usual, the class spent a good deal of time reading and enjoying this book for its literary value. Then students talked about the larger issues of endangered animals and the results of these feisty women's work. After reading the story, the class discussed the environmental issues and the mathematics involved.

MS. BROWN: What is the message of this story?

KATRINA: Don't kill birds, because you can never get them back.

BRAD: You shouldn't kill birds for fashion.

MS. BROWN: What do you think this has to do with mathematics?

JOSEPH: All the different kinds of birds, and the numbers of bird species.

RACHEL: There was lots of subtracting because the birds were dying.

SADE: Minna counted how many birds on hats she saw on the way to her cousin's house.

MS. BROWN: What kinds of problem-solving strategies do you think that Minna and Harriet used?

JOSIE: They first gathered information by looking in the social register, and sent out letters to ask people to stop wearing those hats. Then after they got enough people they had to get some men to go and help make it a law.

BEN: When they went into the shop to pretend to buy a hat so they could trick the owners into giving them their warehouse location, it was kind of like doing a similar problem. In order to catch the people who sold illegal feathers they had to break the law to buy a hat.

MS. BROWN: We are going to begin a mathematical investigation today that will simulate bird extinction. We are not going to use real birds because that would endanger them. We are going to do a simulation that will explore "what would happen if . . ." you killed birds for fashion or destroyed their habitat. Your job will be to sort and classify bird species. You will record your data, graph the results of your simulation, and write about what happened in the simulation. How do you think we might do this?

STEPHANIE: We can use pictures, or we can use an object, or maybe us in place of the birds.

Each two-person team was given a bag of candy (we used one-third of a cup per group) in a variety of assorted colors and shapes (such as Jelly Bellys, M&Ms, and Skittles) to represent bird species. We varied the amounts of candy so that some species were more rare than others. The team's job was to put the candy in groups (in this case species), give the species a name, and record the number they had of each. After they were finished with the sorting the students were asked to look at their data and make a prediction, "Based on the number of the birds in each of your groups, which one of your bird species do you think will become extinct first?"

A thirty-six box grid with a six-by-six matrix and recording sheet were distributed to the pairs. Each box was numbered in a countdown fashion from thirty-six through one starting in the upper left-hand corner. Each of the thirty-six boxes represents one acre of forested land. The students remixed their sorted candy together and spread it out in an even distribution over the grid paper. Each "round" consisted of the students acting out the role of a woodcutter sawing down the forest one acre (or one grid box) at a time. To show the results of the removal of the trees, the birds in that box were eliminated, demonstrating the long-term impact of the destruction of their homes.

The recording sheet has a list of numbers from thirty-six to one with a space next to each. At the conclusion of each round, the students were to count the number of species that had been lost. If they started with twenty-four total species, they looked to see if a round of tree removal had reduced that number (i.e., if they started with ten green M&Ms and now they had none). If no species were lost, they recorded twenty-four next to the line marked to show what happened as the first of the thirty-six acres was eliminated. On the other hand if some species were lost, they record twenty-three, and so on, to keep track of the remaining groups. Many of the students crossed out the actual species' names, as they were rendered extinct.

Next the teams removed the pieces of candy from the box numbered thirty-five in the grid, and checked again for lost species. They continued clearing spaces, one at a time, subtracting for each extinction. When they had cleared the last acre they should have been down to zero species.

Using data obtained from their hunting and clearing expedition, students examined the pattern of loss and graphed it on a stat-plot. On a standard coordinate grid they marked the x-axis with the number of the grid spaces from thirty-six written closest to the origin all the way to one. The number of bird species was represented by the y-axis, which was marked with a one closest to the origin up to the total number of species the pairs originally counted in their collection.

Students will have varied results, but after most teams cleared the first half of the grid spaces, one-fourth to one-third of the species were lost. The extinction rate increased rapidly as the second half was cleared. Students made connections by pointing out that if this fashion movement had gone uncontested, it would have increased the extinction rate of many more species. In the course of the investigation, students became familiar with names of endangered and threatened bird populations. They were particularly interested in a recent article from the local paper, which included information about a family of peregrine falcons who had nested on a bridge spanning the Ohio River. Additional research was encouraged and conducted to locate names of other endangered birds such as the bald eagle, the loon, and the osprey.

This activity allowed for multiple assessments. First we wanted to assess the students' ability to collect, record, and display data accurately in order to draw conclusions. Second, we were assessing their ability to communicate what they were able to do mathematically with the task. In order to evaluate the students' ability to make real-world connections, we also asked them to propose ways to protect and care for local birds and wildlife. This assessment resulted in the students writing informative articles to the Audubon Society explaining what they had investigated, researched, and inferred.

Our analysis of the children's work showed that, as expected, the students were at many different levels in their abilities to communicate what they knew, to explain what puzzled them, to see patterns, and to evaluate strategies. This analysis showed us that the students would need additional opportunities to use stat-plots and evaluate data for similarities and differences.

The class revisited this activity in January when an article about the Annual Audubon Society Christmas Bird Count appeared in the newspaper. The children talked about the counting that is done during a small window of time near Christmas in every state in the nation. Within a fifteen-mile radius of our city 28,662 birds were counted. As a connection to number sense we asked students to think about the number 28,662. "If we wanted to find 28,662 of something in the school, what would it be?" Their first thought was books, but with more reflection and discussion they suggested that the pages in the books, cinder blocks, and floor tiles would be more reasonable answers. We could see that the data could lead to rich mathematical activities.

The students can be provided with other chances to collect real-world data by having them conduct their own bird count for an hour near their home and make predictions of the number of birds in our area. An additional book that can be used in conjunction with this activity is Louise Erdrich's *Grandmother's Pigeon*, a beautiful story that also touches on the topic of the extinction of bird species.

A Mathemagical Day—Incorporating Rubrics

What if you woke up one morning and found yourself in the middle of a math teacher's curse that takes you on a series of wild and crazy mathematical journeys? Jon Scieszka's *Math Curse* does just that to a girl in Mrs. Fibonacci's class. For one day the young girl in the story finds mathematics in every corner of her life. She moves headlong through the day using innovative problem solving to face situations such as dividing cupcakes among class members and locating escape routes that involve halves and "holes." We chose *Math Curse* as a way to assess a student's ability to find mathematical errors.

Our children were astounded at the number and variety of ways that mathematics can be identified within everyday life. After the first reading of the story, the children had many comments and questions concerning the mathematics.

"Sometimes I forget that telling time is math."
"Are all of those real ways to count?"
"We did fractions with pizza pieces before!"
"I never thought adding two words together into a compound word was math."

At this point we heard through an Internet source that there was a mathematical mistake in the book. No one knew exactly what the error was but we decided to put student detectives on the case. Before reading the story the second time, we asked the students to not only focus on the accuracy of the mathematics in the story, but also to find any mathematical connections to reading books, studying at school, playing at home, observing the world around them, and communicating with others. Many students had the opportunity to reread the story individually, examine the illustrations, and discuss it with their friends before the second reading, so they were anxious to share what they knew and to search for the mistake.

Comments after the second reading included, "I talked with my mom about the different ways they showed counting in the book, and she showed me Roman numerals, which is a way to write numbers." "I looked up some statistics in the Guinness Book of World Records on Babe Ruth to see if the numbers in the book were really true." "Are all those real problems or did the author just make them up?"

These comments and the search for the error led naturally to a discussion of assessing another person's work and the strategies that might be used to identify and analyze mistakes. The class was divided into groups of three and assigned a double-page layout from the book. The assignment focused on allowing students to *think* independently, *pair* together in threes to discuss, debate, and decide, and then *share* their findings with the larger group.

The criteria for this task were to examine the pages and make a connection between the mathematics on the page and the real world, to check for mathematical errors, to identify the mathematics concepts, and to find evidence of familiar problems. The groups were given chart paper on which to record their findings and to show creatively what they discovered about their math curse. The group presentations highlighted what they had discovered in looking at their pages:

> *Group 1:* We had the "I wake up at 7:15" page. We drew a clock on our chart paper to show that in the real world we have to know how to tell time and figure out how long we can stay in bed and still get ready on time for school. Kids also want to know when their favorite TV programs are going to be on, and what time they have to get to soccer or baseball practice. We didn't find any math mistakes, but we don't think there is just one answer for the question about teeth. People of different ages would have different amounts of teeth. We think that this page is just about adding and subtracting time and estimating the number of teeth in your mouth.

> *Group 4:* We are the "Stick out your tongue" page. We found lots of math on this page. We drew some of the things that we knew about on our chart like Roman numerals, ticket stubs, musical notes, the globe with latitude and longitude grid lines, rulers, and addition problems. We showed on our chart how many ears, fingers, and tongues are in our class. Today we have twenty-six tongues, fifty-two ears and 260 fingers in the class. The math on this page has counting by twos, fives, or tens. In the desk problem the girl had to find the factors of twenty-four.

Following the discoveries and presentations on *Math Curse*, students were given a task that would assess their ability to find and explain mistakes in a story problem scenario. The problem had to be challenging so that we were reaching the students at both ends of the performance spectrum. In this case the school was raising money to build a log cabin classroom on school grounds. The students were selling books to raise funds for the project. The task was designed to review multiplication and place value concepts. The problem contained several mistakes such as miscopying a number, choosing an incorrect operation, and place value errors. A specific rubric was designed to assess their performance in finding, correcting, and explaining the mathematics.

The assessment rubric aids in defining exactly what we are trying to understand about the students' level of mathematical understanding. A rubric should be precise and provide specific information about the expected proficiency of the child's mathematics at each benchmark. The rubric for this task stated the number of errors and the types of mistake to be found. Frequently our rubrics go through a revision process as we review the student work the first time and find unexpected responses. Often we make adjustments to the wording on the rubric, so there is less room for interpretation.

The five-level rubric we used is both quantitative and qualitative. For example, a score of "three" on this particular rubric indicates a student response correctly identifying three or four computational and place value errors. The student can explain at least three, but has minor errors in mathematical thinking.

The student work provides an avenue for us to examine their processing skills and to see what they are successfully retaining and using. Caitlin observed how the data from the problem was inaccurately recorded when she wrote, "Mallory wrote down fifteen books in the first problem when she only sold five books." Jessica states that when Mallory was adding, she did not line up her numbers, so she did not get the right answer. Jessica's work focused on the concept of place value, and showed the correct alignment in her revised computation. She had most of the ingredients for a score of four on the rubric, but she made a computational error in addition.

A successful scoring rubric provides us with data from students' work that sheds light on their strengths and needs. Martha wrote, "Mallory solved the problem right without any mistakes. The way I figure, you would add 'the Grand total' and the other three totals and that made the grandest total of all." Martha did not even look at the individual computations and thereby provided us with a strong message that she needed more experience in how to read and interpret problems with errors. Instructionally, it would be valuable to review the task with Martha and find out how she arrived at her conclusion.

In contrast, Jamie was so confident of her performance that she wanted us to read her paper as soon as she finished (see Figure 5–1).

In her work Jamie shows that she was able to identify the errors, explain her thinking, and correct the mistakes that were made. Jamie's clear detailing of the mathematical errors and her own accurate computations gave us a broader view of her skill level than could be achieved through observation. The rubric helped us focus on her ability to recognize obvious and subtle errors.

All of the students certainly felt a connection to the character in *Math Curse*

Wheeler School sold paper back books to raise money for the school Log Cabin project. Mallory sold 5 books at $9 each, 11 books at $6 each and 16 at $7 each.

To find out how much money she had to collect, she worked out the following problem on a sheet of paper.

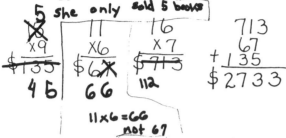

Mallory figured that she would have to collect $2733. Tell whether Mallory solved the problem correctly. If she did not, identify each of her mistakes, and correct her work. Use words numbers or pictures to explain your answer. _Please show all your work_.

1. she said at the top of the page that she sold 5 books for $9 each. She put an her sheet of paper 15 books when it was 5. So she collected $45

2. It also said that she sold 11 books at $6 she came up with $67 but 11 x 6 = 66 dollars not $67.

3. The last answere is rong because the other two are rong so she should come up with this.

$$\begin{array}{r} 5 \\ \times 9 \\ \hline \$45 \end{array} \quad + \begin{array}{r} 11 \\ \times 6 \\ \hline \$66 \end{array} \quad + \begin{array}{r} 16 \\ \times 7 \\ \hline \$112 \end{array} \quad \begin{array}{r} 45 \\ 66 \\ \times 112 \\ \hline \$223 \end{array}$$

She should come up with $223

FIGURE 5–1 _Jamie's assessment of the Log Cabin task_

during their research, presentations, and assessment task. They used mathematical tools they may not have used before, interviewed adults and other students who might have the mathematical knowledge about their particular problems, and incorporated researching skills for mathematics in ways they normally use for science and social studies.

The Volume of Volumes: Assessing Our Teaching

The Library, by Sarah Stewart, is the account of Elizabeth Brown, who is a passionate lover of books and who gives a new meaning to the word "collector." Before even reading a single word the students wanted to make predictions about the girl on the book's cover whose face is completely buried in a book. Libby said, "I guess she just loves to read, because she has just about a million books." Tadd commented that the character "looks like a human encyclopedia."

When we read the story the students found through delightful rhyming verses that Elizabeth has so many books that her shelves are collapsing and she can no longer locate her front door. After many years, she makes an important decision that allows everyone to benefit from her dedication to the written word. After the first reading, Mykel said, "I think the message is if you can get too much of something you collect, it can become a problem." Josie chimed right in, "I think we are going to do an activity that has to do with the average number of books in Elizabeth's collection." Josie was close in her prediction as this story was chosen as a backdrop to assess estimation strategies.

We reminded students about a contest the school had participated in during the past that challenged students to estimate how many shoes it would take to fill a classroom. You not only had to submit a guess, but you had to demonstrate that mathematics was used to find the solution. Some children immediately made the connection and jumped to the conclusion that the class was going to solve a similar problem using books. We divided the students into "think tank" teams and gave them directions through a mathematical prompt.

Students shifted into their groups and started planning estimation strategies. Using the model of a cubic meter, several teams moved to the bookshelves and tested how many books would cover the base of the open cube. Another team grabbed metersticks and measured the length of the classroom. Seeing Courtney's use of the meterstick, we stopped her and asked her to explain her strategy. She suggested correctly that in order to find the volume they needed to measure the length, width, and height of the room.

Each team approached this problem from a different vantage point. We watched as students documented, step-by-step, their process on chart paper. As the students completed the calculations they were anxious to present their findings. As they shared their solutions, we began to realize that there were problems with their measurements. Group after group had mixed units of measure. Some students expressed the length of the room as seven meters and fifteen inches while others mentioned the height of the room as three meters and three inches. When asked to explain how they collected their data, their explanations indicated that they knew to measure in meters for longer distances, but equated the use of the inch with smaller distances. Unfortunately, they incorporated these mixed-unit measurements in their multiplication problems to calculate the volume of the classroom. We also found that they associated the volume of the room with the actual number of books they thought would fill the room, instead of figuring how many books fit into each cubic meter. The assessment quickly showed that the students needed more measuring activities with standard and metric units before the concepts would be internalized. With this knowledge, we made a decision to revisit this particular problem later in the year to see if the students would stand by their original estimates. Between this initial point and our next attempt we would extend students' command of the tools and expand their knowledge of the measuring process.

Later in the year, after many additional measurement experiences, the old pages of calculations were pulled out of students' math portfolios for reexamination and discussion.

> Ms. Brown: Earlier this year we read a book called *The Library* and we are going to look back at the story and our investigation today. Can you recall the mathematics?
>
> Matthew: The mathematical part of the book would be the number of books she had collected over the years.
>
> Becky: She had so many books that she lost count of how many she had.
>
> Courtney: I remember that we did a project about volume, and how many books it would take to fill up this room. We didn't have the right calculations and said 1,000 books would fill up our room. I don't think that would even fill up one fourth of this room.
>
> Ms. Brown: At that time, you gave me a strong message that I needed to give you more opportunities with measuring volume. Since then, we have worked with other estimating strategies, like sampling. How might we use that technique to help us find out approximately how many books will fit in this room?
>
> Matthew: If we took a box as a sample and figured out how many books would fit in one box, then maybe we could figure it out from there.
>
> Ms. Brown: Tell me more about that strategy. How would you use this cubic-foot box?
>
> Josie: First, we need to find out how many of those boxes would fill our room.
>
> Ms. Brown: You are on the right track. What else could we do or use to help us figure this out?
>
> Courtney: We've used the tiles before as one-foot squares.
>
> Ms. Brown: Yes, we have one-foot tiles right at our feet. You will be able to use the tiles to take measurements of the classroom. Will tiles work for the height?
>
> Josie: No, the tiles are only on the floor. The cement blocks are eight inches in width, that might help find the height of the room.

The teams reconvened, examined the task again, and began to count tiles with measured footsteps to find the width and length of the classroom. One team counted the cement blocks and was multiplying to find the height. We had only one cubic-foot box to use as the sample, so teams used rulers and books for models placing the rulers in one-foot squares on the table and stacking books one foot high. As we watched, listened, and questioned we saw them using what they had learned about sampling. Instead of equating the estimate of books as the number of square feet in the room, they were now filling a consistent unit with books and then using that as a unit of measurement.

Each group developed a presentation about their strategies and results. The new presentations showed a much higher level of conceptual understanding. The following represents a verbal snapshot from one of the presentations:

> The title of our chart is How Many Books Will Fill Our Classroom? Our estimation was 292,900 books. That was our guess. We figured out there really could be 92,736 books in our classroom. We figured out our answer by finding out how many books could fit in a cubic foot. We came up with fourteen books. The length of the room was thirty-two feet, the width was twenty-three feet, and the height was nine feet. We multiplied these numbers to get the volume, which was 6,624 cubic feet, then multiplied by fourteen because fourteen books filled the one foot square box. We came up with 92,736 books.

Each group was able to show the use of efficient strategies in determining the estimates. The final activity was to put the estimates in order from least to greatest, to find the mean, median, mode, and range, and to write about what they discovered doing the same activity a second time by comparing the new estimations to their original work. Kendra noted that there was a mode of 92,736 in the new estimations as that number occurred twice. Jill said that she didn't remember any numbers this high the first time the class estimated. Matthew agreed and said he thought that this time we did a better job of measuring. Alex said that his group was on the right track last time, but the cubic foot was easier to sample than the cubic meter.

In reflecting on our work, we found that initially we had not accurately assessed the students' background knowledge in order to know if they could be successful in finding estimates for volume. These not-so-successful instructional activities are as important to our learning as making mistakes are to our students' learning of mathematics. This "curriculum assessment" process reminded us to gauge carefully what students bring to each lesson and to carefully observe how they are able to apply that knowledge.

Kindred Spirits: Interviewing

"The problem is . . . we don't have enough money," explains Mountain Girl to her family, as she tries to impress upon them her desire to have more of the material possessions that her friends have. *The Table Where Rich People Sit*, by Byrd Baylor, gives us a unique chance to make connections between mathematics, values, and real life. Mountain Girl, who is quick to take leadership in bringing her family to a meeting to discuss her thoughts, is mathematically correct in her understanding of the cost of the material items in her home. But her family takes the time to patiently teach her the value of the life around her. Her parents describe themselves as paid in sunsets and in the changing colors of the mountains, the sight of the eagle, and the smell of the wind and the rain. Her father suggests that it is worth twenty thousand dollars to him to work outdoors. Mountain Girl's mother adds, "You'd better make that thirty thousand because it's worth at least another ten to hear coyotes howling back in the hills."

In sharing this story students began to appreciate how valuable the environment around them is, and they sensed the value of the family members to one another. It was through this connection that a task was given to the students that would allow them to discover the monetary "value" of the chores that families do for each other in the course of a weekend. Recognizing that family members complete most household chores without pay, we wanted the children to see what it might cost if they had to hire someone outside the family to do the work. Our assessment focus in this task was to examine computation strategies, data organization, and interpretation.

Networking groups first had to identify the ten most necessary jobs families accomplish on a given weekend. Groups brainstormed ideas and shared them with the rest of the class to create a master list of tasks. Second, the groups had to determine the monetary value of each job. This aspect of the problem was discussed in class and then taken home and shared with their families for feedback. At a subsequent class meeting, the students decided that they should use the minimum wage established by the government to calculate the hourly jobs. They also discovered that some jobs have a fixed fee according to the "going rate" in their areas. Lawn mowing, for example, was a job where a single amount is charged depending on the area of the property.

Students created glyphs to record data they collected from home. A backdrop of a mountain was used as the basis for the glyph with the key symbols incorporating the drawings from Mountain Girl's story such as the table, the sun, a tree, and the cabin. Each symbol represented a job accomplished at home by a family member.

The first part of the task required the children to collect data about any household chores family members performed over the weekend. The children created forms that would indicate the kind and duration of the jobs. Some children used tallies to mark the quarter hours, half hours, and full hours spent, others kept lists of completed chores accomplished, while some students created elaborate narrative methods of recording the information.

The glyphs were completed with the information brought back to class and were helpful in organizing the data. After preparing individual glyphs, students compared them within small groups, writing statements representative of the findings of their team. Comments from students indicated an awareness that the glyph could only record types of chores actually completed, but could not tell how many hours were worked or the monetary value of the work done. Desiree's comments about her glyph showed her understanding about the purpose of a glyph (see Figure 5–2).

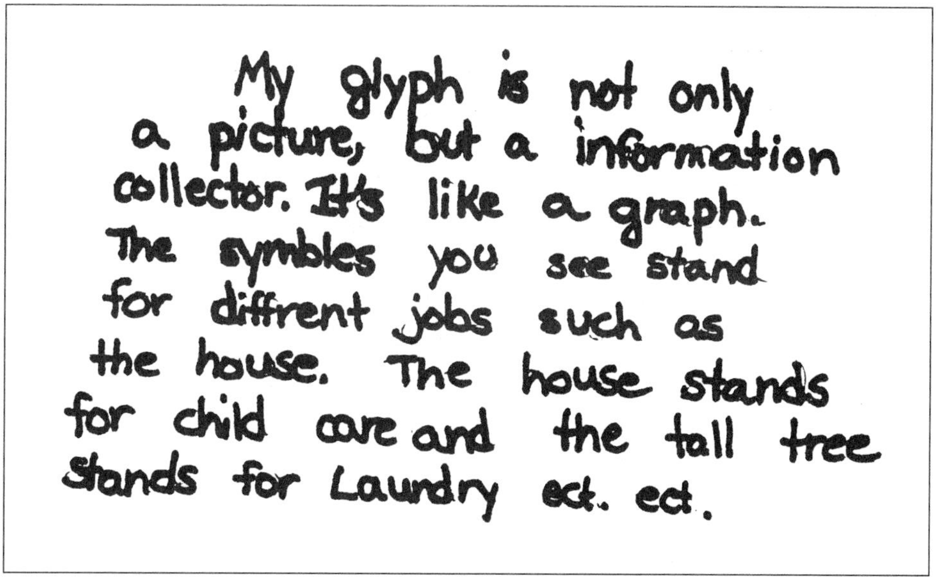

FIGURE 5–2   *Desiree's glyph comment*

Individually, students had to calculate the monetary value for each job recorded in their chart. A variety of strategies was used to determine the cost of a twenty-minute job when the pay was given based on an hourly figure. Some children rounded the exact time up or down so that they could deal with more "workable" numbers. Others were able to find the value of fractional parts of the hour, and used this proportion as a calculating figure. Discussions of the processes used were important not only in the connections with the real world, but also in assessing what the children knew and could do.

A group of four children were brought together in a group interview to work out the mathematics of this problem.

MS. ALLEN: Explain your task for me.

MEGAN: The problem we had to figure out is how many dollars our families saved by doing the jobs over the weekend ourselves.

JAMESON: We needed to know the dollar value of the work. I can't remember how we decided that.

MS. ALLEN: Can you explain to Jameson how we decided on the dollar value of a job?

MEGAN: It means if another person who's not in our family did it, how much would they get paid. Mostly it is minimum wage which is about $5.50 an hour. Six dollars an hour is what we usually round it to so we can make the math easier.

SEAN: Now we need to figure the cost for each job. We can multiply the $6 times the number of hours that the job took.

MS. ALLEN: How can we decide on the value of a job that does not take a full hour to do?

SEAN: Thirty minutes is half the time so we would earn $3 because it's half of $6.

MEGAN: Wait, what if they only work twenty minutes or ten minutes? If there are sixty minutes in an hour, then every ten minutes would be worth $1. That makes it easier to figure out.

MS. ALLEN: Megan, explain how that works.

MEGAN: If you draw a clock you can mark off ten minutes all the way around it and you'd have six groups of ten in one hour. It's one dollar for every group.

This short inquiry interview helped us see that Megan had a good understanding of the problem, that Sean knew how to use his multiplication, and that all four children relied on one another in practical ways. The children continued to work independently to figure the costs of each chore completed over the weekend.

On another day the children were again asked to "think about their thinking" and begin reflecting on the work accomplished. Focus questions were given to structure their responses. They included:

1. Explain why you collected the data.
2. How did your group decide the value of an hour's work?
3. How did you calculate how much your family "earned" for each job?
4. How did you calculate the value of all the work your family completed over the weekend?
5. Explain what information your glyph tells about your family.

Students were advised to include examples of their mathematics in the writing. We encouraged them to reflect, write, build in examples, reflect some more, and continue with their math writing. In small groups children continued to talk together and support one another in sorting out the language needed to convey their understandings. Sometimes the talk seemed confusing to the adult interviewer, but the sharing of ideas and information enabled students to make that particular concept part of their own knowledge base.

MS. ALLEN: What did you learn by doing this task?

MEGAN: I think we found out that we could save a lot of money by doing the jobs in our family, instead of paying someone else.

SEAN: What about child care? Some groups were figuring out child care like when our parents take care of us.

MACKENZIE: But what about the nights when we're sleeping? That shouldn't be part of the child care.

JAMESON: Yes, it is. What if you're sick? My dad comes to check on me in the night in case I'm sick.

MACKENZIE: But that shouldn't matter.

JAMESON: Well, it should matter! He has to watch me at night, so I want it to count.

MS. ALLEN: Jameson, if you include nighttime child care, what would its value be?

JAMESON: Over the weekend, it's thirty-six hours at $6 an hour. Let me figure it out. That's $216.

SEAN: Wow, that's a lot for taking care of us.

The children continued to discuss how to find the value of individual jobs and then to find the grand total of all the jobs completed at home. As the dialogue became more reflective children thought about their special wealth, the work they do for others, and how much their parents contribute to their lives. As the project ended and reflections were written, we were able to note several comments on each child's work in anecdotal records. MacKenzie, although quiet in a large group, was able to explain her thinking and take a position on an idea within her small group. Also, we observed and noted the give-and-take between two leaders who ended up in the same cooperative group.

Discovering the strengths and needs children have during this type of assessment is the power of embedded assessment. Merely assessing products in isolation furnishes only one small sample of the students' work. Examining the cooperation between members, the students' organizational abilities, their skill in planning, and their oral and written communication skills become other key ingredients in the bigger picture. Oftentimes success in the workplace is tied not to superior test-taking skills but to working well with others. For the classroom to be an authentic preparation for the future, we found we must help students develop strengths on several levels. We recognize all too well that our assessments send a very clear message of what we value.

Works Cited

POLLINA, ANN. 1995. "Gender Balance: Lessons from Girls in Science and Mathematics." *Educational Leadership* 53 (1) 30–33.

Children's Literature

BAYLOR, BYRD. 1994. *The Table Where Rich People Sit.* New York: Charles Scribner's Sons Books for Young Readers.

ERDRICH, LOUISE. 1996. *Grandmother's Pigeon.* New York: Hyperion Books for Children.

LASKY, KATHRYN. 1995. *She's Wearing a Dead Bird on Her Head!* New York: Hyperion Books for Children.

SCIESZKA, JON. 1995. *Math Curse.* New York: Penguin Books.

STEWART, SARAH. 1995. *The Library.* New York: Farrar, Straus & Giroux.

6

Inventing Solutions

Because of the ways females are socialized, one area they tend to have difficulty with is higher-level problem solving. While one of their strengths is in following rules generated by an authority, a pervasive area of weakness is in taking chances and risks. For girls to become independent learners, they must learn to take a leadership role in their own education, face challenging problems without continuous approval from an authority figure, persevere, guess, and develop a questioning disposition.

The NCTM puts problem solving as standard 1, signifying that this process should permeate all mathematics instruction. They see a good problem solver as being flexible and fluent in moving from words to images to symbols and from mathematical concepts to mathematical content in the real world. They can identify a variety of methods to reach solutions and can see patterns in all that they do.

In 1989 the National Academy of Sciences and the National Council of Teachers of Mathematics took strong stands for a problem-solving focus in teaching and against the emphasis on student learning through the absorption of formulas and procedures. This type of blind compliance both hinders critical thinking and restricts the development of logical reasoning skills. When mathematics is presented as rule-based and procedure-centered, the skills necessary for higher level thinking are neglected (Fennema and Peterson 1985). This finding is further complicated because formula dependency has been identified as a contributing factor in females' mathematics difficulties.

It has been suggested that female elementary students become more dependent on their teachers as a result of identifying with them, following their rules precisely, and seeking frequent approval. Although these behavior patterns reap rewards in the early years of schooling, they impede females' development of autonomous learning styles, which are critical for acquiring abstract mathematical concepts. Additionally, female students have been found to be more dependent on feedback from external sources such as teachers to assess their performance (Dweck, Davidson, Nelson, and

Enna 1978). This need for external endorsement promotes an attitude of dependence in female students who are functioning in a system that rewards initiative.

Learned Helplessness

The teacher-student dependency created through these behaviors is of particular concern, as it encourages a learned helplessness in the female student population. Learned helplessness is the perception that you need help from others and that others will do the thinking for you. In classroom settings it can be seen to be a likely consequence when a student encounters failure and views her own effort as irrelevant in affecting future outcomes, or when a teacher does most of the thinking for the student in an effort to be helpful and the student learns to wait for assistance instead of plunging into the task. Students who have developed this "learned helplessness syndrome" attribute problems in mathematics to factors they see as either unchangeable or uncontrollable, such as their ability, the difficulty of the task, or the response of other people. As John Van de Walle states, "Good mathematics is not how many answers you know, but how you behave when you do not know" (1997).

This may lead females to internalize the belief that they cannot do mathematics tasks independently. Males' achievement in mathematics was not affected by the ease or frequency of help, but females did better with less help and actually withholding help seemed beneficial (Koehler 1990). Affirming that conclusion, Leder's (1990) work shows the group with the most "helping" interactions with the teacher was the females with the lowest performance in mathematics. In both cases, less teacher monitoring was found to help encourage independent thinking skills. We caution that although students should receive less teacher help in some cases, we do not want them to become isolated leaders on the path to being more independent learners. Some additional advice on this issue comes from Carolyn Burke (1995) who suggests, "Don't step in front of the struggle."

This chapter centers on the use of motivating problem-solving activities, situations where novel solutions are encouraged, and ways to create investigations for independent learning experiences. We have attempted to include problems that require insight, reason, inventiveness, risk taking, and mathematical proficiency.

Choosing Wisely

In the book *Cinder Edna*, by Ellen Jackson, the main character is a good example of a problem solver. Here is a story of two young females, told in a style that moves back and forth from one character to the other throughout the book. One female is the renowned Cinderella who faces the tasks set by her stepmother and stepsisters with sadness and the traditional sympathy-provoking actions that we're familiar with. Her tale is contrasted with the life of her feisty neighbor, Cinder Edna, who, in response to the challenges she is given, discovers how to "get spots off everything from rugs to ladybugs" and who can "make tuna casserole sixteen different ways." While Cinderella has her fairy godmother fashion a carriage and outfit for her to wear to the ball, Cinder Edna tackles the same situation on her own by using saved money to put a dress on layaway, wearing loafers, and taking the bus. This humorous parody enables readers to contrast two different problem-solving styles. The students contrasted the "old-fashioned" behaviors of Cinderella to her 1990s counterpart. Yet more important mathematically, the differences reinforce the possibilities of multiple problem-solving strategies. Hence, this book can lead to a look at nonroutine problems and a variety of approaches for solutions.

Children may understand the meaning of certain words, but that does not ensure that they can interpret these terms in a mathematical context. Many students need to write their own problems to become more fluent in this process. The steps we use in getting them to write their own problems are:

1. Teacher gives an example
2. Students brainstorm ideas
3. Students create stories, questions, and solutions
4. Students meet in small groups called forums where they use peer conferencing
5. Students showcase problems in either "From the Mathematician's Chair" or a publication of mathematics problems to go home to families.

Using the story line of *Cinder Edna*, we decided to give students the task of creating their own problem-solving situations. We started by noting that Cinder Edna is able to make a tuna casserole in numerous ways. In response to that focus on her capacity to be resourceful, we gave the students a problem that could be solved with several different strategies. We suggested that Cinder Edna could add any combination of three of the following four ingredients to the tuna and noodle mixture: peas, onions, celery, and mushrooms. Using any combination of three vegetables, we asked how many different ways could she make a tuna casserole?

After making an estimate as to what they thought would be the outcome, the third- and fourth-grade students discussed within their groups different strategies that could be used to find the exact number of combinations. Some groups wanted to act it out with candy pieces as representations of the vegetables, while others wanted to make a table. Several students started using small illustrations of the four ingredients, or actual pieces of similarly colored goodies to represent the various choices. As they tested various combinations, many students successfully identified patterns, but several decided the strategies they had chosen weren't as efficient as they had previously thought. "This table is getting me all confused. I can't tell which combinations I have and which ones I'm missing," commented one student. "Putting the candy in combinations is too slow," lamented another child.

Groups started sharing with each other, and a few students mentioned that making a list would help them get organized. Many students eventually changed from their initial strategy to trying an approach that included an organized list.

As they tested various combinations the children began to identify patterns and came up with many ways to organize the possibilities. Students also asked questions as to how results would change if they only used two ingredients at a time or if cashews were added as another possible ingredient. Of course those ideas led to investigations of other number variations and patterns.

The most difficult part of the problem-solving activity was answering the question, "How do you know you have found all the possible combinations?" The students answers ranged from "I just thought and thought and couldn't think of anything else" to "I was very organized and did all the combinations with three ingredients, then four, then five, and then six, and then I found a pattern and knew there couldn't be any more."

Then it was the students' turn to brainstorm new scenarios for additional problems. A second reading of the story provided a chance to highlight the different types of mathematical situations that could be found in the book. Before beginning the mathematics task, the students reviewed some of the wisdom identified in the story at an earlier reading.

MS. ALLEN: What were some of the mathematical situations that we found in the story of Cinder Edna?

SEAN: The story tells about how much money people get paid in an hour.

SARAH: You have to know about math to make the recipes for the banquet food.

MS. ALLEN: These situations are excellent examples of using mathematics in the real world.

The task was defined by explaining that each student would construct a problem-solving situation based on the story line of Cinder Edna. Our initial criteria were that it had to be connected to the story in some way and it had to be a mathematical situation. The first question the students asked was "Can we do any kind of math problem?" We assured them that any type of problem could be designed, any strategy could be used to solve it, and any mathematics concepts could be the focus. The class talked together and created a list on the board of problem types such as combinations, computation, and data gathering; problem-solving strategies such as working backward, multiple step, and making a table; and content such as fractions, geometry, and algebraic thinking. Many students were overwhelmed with the "choices," but we assured them that they would be able to include all these components once their math imaginations started operating.

We asked the students to take time to do some silent thinking about one or two problem-solving situations that they could see happening within the story. They were to jot down in their journals any ideas during this "think" time that might lead them to creating a problem. After the "think" time, students were asked to pair up and discuss their preliminary ideas. Then as a whole group, we listened to several ideas from each table. As an assignment, the children were to share with their parents their initial problem and to talk it through before the next class.

In returning to the problem-generating process, the students were very motivated and ready to try their problems out. It was at this time that the class suggested that we have a rubric so that they would know what constituted a quality problem. Together the group decided on important criteria and the design of the scoring guide. A group of three children created a visual representation of puzzle pieces coming together to show how well they could perform their tasks.

Children worked for several days developing the problem situations, testing possible strategies, seeing if they could explain how to help others solve their problems, working with peer groups for revising, and sharing nightly with their parents. A few days after the students designed the scoring rubric and began working on their individual problems, the group gathered together as a whole class to act as a revising board.

> MS. ALLEN: Let's look at the rubric that you created this week for our Cinder Edna problems. I really liked the way you used a puzzle to show how you progress to understanding the big picture. I see that there are three levels of achievement on your rubric. The first level would be marked if certain parts of the problem you created show that you don't quite understand the criteria; the second level shows some understanding; and the third level lets us know that your problem shows a clear understanding of the criteria.

Several students were invited to sit in forums and share their problems with a group. As the author shares the draft of the problem orally, the students are ready to share strengths and weaknesses. All students have a pad of small, sticky notes on which to write a "star" and a "wish." The star represents something positive that the author has done, and the wish is something that needs to be improved before the final assessment. The rubric was displayed to remind the other students what they were listening for in each problem. Could they understand the problem and have a sense of what they were to do to solve it? Does the problem involve real mathematical situations? Does the problem relate in some way to *Cinder Edna?* The author collects all the sticky notes on their paper or notebook, and uses the comments when revising their problem. We have the students classify the suggestions so that they can get a sense of what the problem really needs in order to be well done. This sharing gives them an opportunity to reflect on their work and choose from suggestions given by others. At the same time, the author of the problem must be ready to help other children with appropriate clues and suggestions of strategies.

In one group Megan reads her problem aloud and then gives the students a few minutes of thinking and writing time to solve the problem and critique her work. Some sharing of the strengths and weaknesses is important to do aloud in order to give students an opportunity to hear positive comments and helpful suggestions.

> MEGAN: Rupert tripped over Randolph's foot and fell. His glasses fell off, broke, and little pieces of glass scattered everywhere. Your task is to estimate how many pieces of glass are on the ground [shown in a picture she has included]. After you finish estimating, explain how you got your answer.

MS. ALLEN: We need to share ideas that will help Megan revise her problem. I would like for some of you to share what you wrote on your sticky note to Megan.

DESIREE: I have a strength for Megan. I like the way that her problem is about Rupert's glasses falling off at midnight at the ball. That was a good connection to the story.

SARAH: I'm not sure that there is more than one way to solve your problem, Megan.

MS. ALLEN: Megan, what can you say to Sarah to justify what you have written in your work?

MEGAN: There are at least two ways to solve it. You can have a group of ten pieces of glass circled and then find how many other groups there are about that size. You can also draw squares around color tiles and estimate what's in one square like what we did with the bug problem this year.

LAUREN: Megan, do you think this problem is challenging enough? I think it might be too easy.

MEGAN: It might be easy for some kids, but some kids might just try to count the pieces and not know how to really estimate them.

Lauren's problem situation centered on Prince Randolph looking for his traditional Cinderella (see Figure 6–1). Cooper and Desiree acted as Lauren's peer team to assess her final product. Both children marked the criteria on one of three levels (see Figure 6–2). We met with Lauren in an interview to talk about her problem.

MS. ALLEN: Lauren, I see that you worked with Cooper and Desiree to assess the math problem you designed about Cinder Edna. Share some of your thoughts with me on the results of their assessment.

LAUREN: All three of us thought my problem was clear in most of the areas. Cooper wasn't sure that it was understandable to an audience, but maybe he didn't know how to work it, because Desiree thought it was understandable.

MS. ALLEN: What do you think, Lauren?

LAUREN: I checked my work to see if I could solve it, and it made sense. It's just a problem that you have to think about.

MS. ALLEN: Did you notice anything else about your assessment?

LAUREN: Cooper and Desiree thought I could have used more power words, and I thought so too, but I really couldn't decide what they would have been.

All three students gave a good assessment of Lauren's work. Lauren's problem was very clear in spite of the fact that she could not work in what she, Cooper, and Desiree thought would be good math vocabulary words to strengthen her "math reliability."

When the children finished revising in their groups, the final event was for some

Prince Randoph was looking
for Cinderella by trying the
glass slipper on the girl feet.
He finished half $(\frac{1}{2})$ of girls feet
that didn't fit. Then he finished
one forth $(\frac{1}{4})$ of the half $(\frac{1}{2})$ He
had 6 left. How many girls did
he start with?
    After you figure this problem
out Explain why you picked what
you picked and how you figured
it out

FIGURE 6-1 *Lauren's* Cinder Edna *problem*

children to share their problem with the entire class from the Mathematician's Chair while others created a class publication of problems that could go home to each family. When the publication was completed, students made the parents a page of problem-solving strategy suggestions as clues and gave them all of the solutions. In this way they thought parents who enjoy examining other possible approaches and answers could see what the "experts" found.

One Hundred Percent Clever

Aunt Skilly and the Stranger, by Kathleen Stevens, is a story about an elderly woman who tends to her cabin on Which-Way Mountain in Appalachia and creates beautiful hand-stitched quilts. One day a stranger appears at her door and shows a great interest in Aunt Skilly's quilts and her surroundings. He asks her the kind of questions that prompt the reader to become concerned for the woman's safety. The reader thinks Aunt Skilly is in grave danger, but the cagey stranger is not as wily as Aunt Skilly.

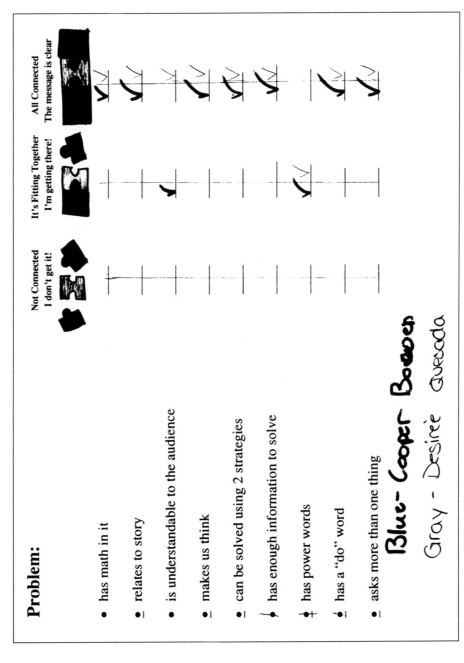

FIGURE 6–2   *Lauren's peer assessment rubric*

The activities that came about from reading this story were generated by mathtalks we had during and after reading the book. Not surprisingly, the story piqued an interest in quilts that led to several activities tied to geometric concepts. The students found a gem of mathematical wisdom that drew our attention to work with fractions and decimals. In a memorable line, Aunt Skilly describes the stranger as being "one part muscle and nine parts fool." Here is how one of our mathtalks went:

Ms. BROWN: What do you think of our predictions about the stranger?

LAUREN: A lot of people were saying that he was a mean stranger and they were right.

Ms. BROWN: What about Aunt Skilly?

SUSIE: She put her quilts in her box and then she put [cornhusks] in the bags and she tricked the stranger.

Ms. BROWN: Did you think as we were reading this story that she knew about the stranger?

JAMIE: Well, if he asked her all those questions, she was bound to know.

Ms. BROWN: Why do you think she was bound to know?

JAMIE: Because if he were a kind stranger he wouldn't go up there and ask her all those strange questions.

ERIC: He always kept on asking her about the quilts and saying they are worth a lot of money.

Ms. BROWN: Where do you think there is mathematics in this story? Where did you hear or see mathematics?

ERIC: The three quilts.

KAMAU: The patterns on the quilts.

JAMIE: The amount of money that he gave her.

LIBBY: The sentence about the stranger being one part muscle and ten parts fool.

Ms. BROWN: I am going to reread the line from the story. "Aunt Skilly heaped a bowl with seed corn and set it on the floor. That stranger was one part muscle and nine parts fool, she said lifting the lid of the wooden chest."

RYAN: I heard one part muscle and nine parts fool.

Ms. BROWN: Can anyone say that using fractions?

LIBBY: He was one-tenth muscle and nine-tenths fool.

Ms. BROWN: We are going to do an activity today that has to do with the parts of you.

This activity became a component of our study of fractional parts. Students had been working with a variety of fractional models, pattern blocks, pie pieces, fractional paper plates, and fraction bars. The purpose of this activity was for them to use their fraction bars as a unit of measure and to think of themselves as having characteristics that are parts of their whole person.

We began by showing them self-portraits. We brainstormed what could be writ-

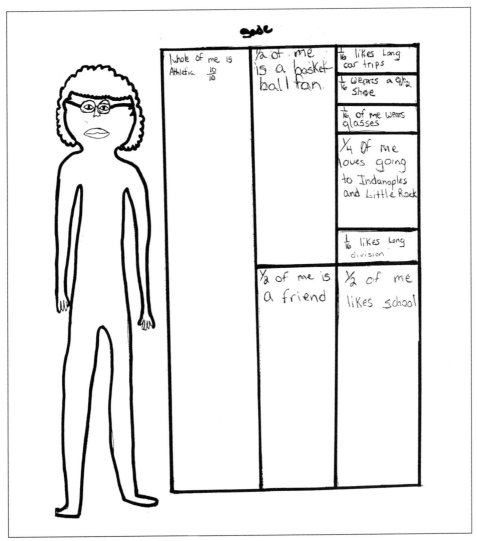

Sade

Whole of me is Athletic $\frac{10}{10}$	$\frac{1}{2}$ of me is a basketball fan.	$\frac{1}{16}$ likes long car trips
		$\frac{1}{16}$ wears a $9\frac{1}{2}$ shoe
		$\frac{1}{16}$ of me wears glasses
		$\frac{1}{4}$ of me loves going to Indanoples and Little Rock
		$\frac{1}{16}$ likes long division
	$\frac{1}{2}$ of me is a friend	$\frac{1}{2}$ of me likes school

FIGURE 6–3   *Sade's fraction portrait*

ten that would describe us in fractional terms, such as one whole, one-half, one-fourth, one-eighth, one-sixteenth. The students suggested that looking at the picture they saw one whole person, one whole female. They said there was one-half upper body, and one-half lower body. They could see that one-sixth was head. Then they began their drawings and writing about themselves. Many students drew their bodies as one-half of the whole, because they felt they were not fully grown. That led to an interesting discussion about what constitutes one whole. Many had to go back and lengthen their bodies to make themselves one whole. This also gave us some very odd looking drawings with disproportionate bodies. Then they wrote about what they discovered about themselves as fractional parts.

Sade and Stephanie approached this problem from different perspectives. Sade looked at her intrinsic qualities, whereas Stephanie wrote about her physical attributes (see Figures 6–3 and 6–4). Sade's fractional model mirrored the way Aunt Skilly saw the stranger.

The Aunt Skilly activity gave students not only a way to apply fraction skills but also an opportunity to look at themselves from another point of view. Some students were only able to see themselves as a whole child, a whole sister, or a whole daughter. Others could describe their body proportions as fractional parts such as "one-sixth head" or "one-half of me walks." Their ability to illustrate and describe themselves in terms of fractions gave us more information about their level of mastery.

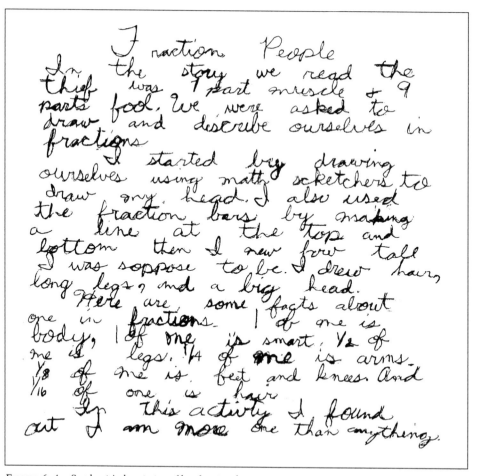

FIGURE 6–4   *Stephanie's description of her fraction drawing*

Going Buggy

Insects Are My Life, by Megan McDonald, describes the life of Amanda Frankenstein, which centers on the creepy crawlers around her. Her life is filled with metaphors, stories, and wonderment about insects and all that they mean. She wrestles with finding understanding within her circle of family and friends because no one seems to be able to appreciate her enthusiasm for bugs. That is, until she meets a friend whose motto is "Reptiles are my life!" McDonald's book was a wonderful way to explore strategies for estimating number.

We read the story twice and after our "math wisdom" discussion students began working on estimating strategies. The children were given a standard eight-and-a-half-by-eleven-inch sheet of paper covered with a random collection of tiny insects and were asked to estimate the number of insects on the page using two or more different strategies. They had a chance to talk to one another about it, to share ideas, to try different approaches, and to compare strategies. We then asked them for the estimates from their first strategy, which were written on the chalkboard.

MS. ALLEN: When we look at a set of data like this, what can we do with this information?

SARAH: We could find the range. We find the lowest estimate and then the highest estimate and the difference is the range. The estimates are 100 to 450. The range is 350. Wow, that's a big difference.

MS. ALLEN: Now look at the estimate you found from using your second strategy. I would like you to think about how your estimates changed from the first strategy to the second. How would you do this?

WESLEY: We subtracted the smaller number from the larger number.

MS. ALLEN: Anna, what was the difference in your two estimates?

ANNA: Sixty-five.

MS. ALLEN: Do you think the difference in Anna's estimate is reasonable?

WESLEY: Her estimates are much closer together than mine. The difference between my estimates was 150.

MS. ALLEN: Why did some of you use a third strategy?

LAUREN: I had to because my first two estimates were so different. I couldn't come up with one answer.

MS. ALLEN: Can one of the teams tell me the first strategy that you used?

WESLEY AND COURTNEY: We divided the whole page into boxes and found the number of boxes on the page by multiplying seven times nine. We counted six bugs in each box and times sixty-three boxes the answer is 378 bugs. But there might be more and there might be less.

MS. ALLEN: What was your next strategy?

COURTNEY AND WESLEY: We counted the number of bugs across the top of the page in the wiggly line [the bugs were in all different orientations] and the number down the page in the wiggly line. We got sixteen across the top and twenty down the side. We multiplied the numbers together and got 320 bugs.

MS. ALLEN: Did anyone get the answer a different way?

KORINE: I used place value pieces. I laid the mats, strips, and ones on top of the entire piece of paper. I figured each little square could hold one bug.

MS. ALLEN: How did you figure out how many insects covered the page?

KORINE: I put all the hundred mats, the ten strips, and the ones together and counted them all up. I got 405 bugs today. I did it yesterday the same way and got 415 bugs. I don't know why it's different.

MS. ALLEN: Korine, think about your work. Did you do anything different today with your strategy than yesterday?

KORINE: I don't know. Well, I might have counted some of the blocks that were hanging off the edge of the paper. Wait, I might have added the blocks together wrong because I also couldn't take the hundred mat apart so if it was hanging off I probably counted the extra too. I didn't think about that!

MS. ALLEN: So far the class has tried three different strategies and the answers are different. Sometimes students have found the answer is different when they use the same strategy more than once. What do mathematicians do when they find different answers to the same problem?

DREW: They keep on trying to find out what the real answer is. They can use another strategy or think about what is wrong with the ones they've already used.

MS. ALLEN: Let's look at the strategy Wesley showed us. She and Courtney counted six bugs in a box and multiplied it by sixty-three boxes on the page. Did anyone use that strategy in a different way?

ANNA: When I was looking at the boxes, some of them had five bugs, some had six bugs and some had eight bugs. So I used all those numbers and multiplied each of them times sixty-three which is the number of boxes. The answers were really different. I found 315 bugs, 378 bugs, and 504 bugs.

MS. ALLEN: As a mathematician Anna had to make a decision on which number to use as the number of bugs in each box. Anna, why did you choose six?

ANNA: I used the number six because it was in the middle.

MS. ALLEN: Anna, when you reflect on your work and write about it, make sure you explain why you tried all those numbers, and why you decided on using the number six as the number of bugs in the box.

Our goal for the students is always to develop positive mathematics attitudes. We want them to be able to feel confident in their basic skills, but most important, we want independent, self-motivated thinkers. We encourage students to develop a wide variety of problem-solving techniques, and help them learn to communicate what they have accomplished by talking with others and by writing their reflections. We want students to feel joy in finding challenges in mathematics. Hopefully some will say, "Mathematics is my life."

The Ultimate Correspondence

What did people ever do before the telephone and e-mail? *The Long, Long Letter,* by Elizabeth Spurr, is a humorous book that answers that question while leading to a data-collection activity and some interesting problem-solving explorations. The story begins with lonely Aunt Hetta sitting beside her mailbox and lamenting that she hasn't received a letter in a while. Her sister knows just what to do. She responds by writing a long letter over several seasons. The delivery of this long correspondence leads to a wonderful surprise.

The book is rich with mathematical connections. In the discussion about the wisdom of the story and the character's problem solving the students were skeptical about the sister being able to write that many pages. Nicholas said that he heard one of the phrases, "writing up a storm," in language class but even writing all the time would not produce that many letters. Alex posed a question about how many pages you would really have if you wrote one page every day of the fall, winter, spring, and summer. They pointed out that although the letters were taken to the post office in six boxes, when the mail fell from the sky it took "three days to gather with snowplows and a tractor." Some thought this was mathematically unreasonable and others wondered how many children it would take to carry that many letters. Brandi speculated that the class might want to check the numbers using sampling techniques on the illustration in the book to try and determine how many letters fell from the sky.

During our mathematical talk Joseph said, "I think I know what we are going to do. I think we are going to tally the amount of mail we get each day." We did a quick survey of the class to see how many people received personal letters on a regular basis. Fewer than ten people raised their hand.

Next, we moved into a conversation about the mail that the students' families receive at home each day. A brainstorming session generated some possible categories of items that might be discovered in an average mailbox. The students were first given think time, then they talked with partners, and finally they shared their ideas with the group. They suggested magazines, catalogues, newsletters, bills, paychecks, letters from friends and relatives, birthday cards, information notices from school, bank information, offers of products (like CD clubs), advertisements, requests for contributions, coupons, and small packages and gifts. From this hefty list the students grouped items into five categories. It took some work, but they decided on the following categories:

Advertisements, which included catalogues, coupons, and store advertisements

Magazines, which included newsletters

Money, which included bills, checks, bank information, charge card information and requests for contributions

Information, which included notices, school announcements, report cards

Letters, which included notes from family and friends, greeting cards, and small
gifts.

We like to limit the students' choices to four or five possibilities having found that
allowing too many options dilutes the data-analysis process. The only time we devi-
ate from this is when the categories demand a greater number (such as in months of
the year).

The children were given a prompt that asked them to do three things. First
they were to estimate how many pieces of mail the entire class would receive in a
week. Then using the five categories, they were to keep a record of all the mail that
came into their home during that week. Finally, they were asked to bring in a representative sample from the one category that had received the greatest number of
in their household that week. If it was awkward for the child to bring in an actual
sample (like a bill or catalogue) we suggested they bring in just the envelope or
cover or a drawing of them. To practice categorizing, several samples of mail were
shown to the class as examples and discussed so that the group would have an
agreed-on standard.

Most of the students predicted Money would be the category with the most mail
collected by the class in a one-week time frame. They each put their sample in a
"mailbag." After they collected the data, the mailbags were dumped on the floor and
sorted into the five categories. The students were then asked to look at their
recorded data and to help construct a graph.

From the sorted piles left on the floor, the children picked up their sample piece
of mail and moved into a large area outside the classroom. They formed groups by
category; the groups then formed a circle with kids representing one category shoulder to shoulder and next to those from another category thus making a continuing
arc of a circle. Using a bicycle gear with five long pieces of clothesline rope knotted
onto the sprocket, we placed the metal cog at the center of the circle. The first string
was passed to the first child in the Advertisements group. By navigating the circle,
we marked each change of group with one of the five strings. What they created was
a circle graph of the data. Because it is difficult to interpret a graph when you are part
of it, they placed their samples on the ground to mark their spots, lowered the strings
to a position on the floor, and stepped back. From there it was easier to analyze the
circle graph.

As the students stood around the circle, we asked them if they had accurately
predicted the category in which they were a part. The final results matched very few
of their predictions.

MS. BROWN: Let's analyze our human graph by using three questions: "What do
you think?," "What do you know?," and "What puzzles you?"

BRAD: I know there were more catalogues and coupons than anything else.

MATTHEW: I know that more people had catalogues mailed to their home in a
week than magazines.

MS. BROWN: Matthew, how did you get your answer?

MATTHEW: I saw the number of people standing in that section took up the most space.

MS. BROWN: Are there any patterns?

MARAT: There were two categories that had two of the twenty-five students. That is the mode.

NICHOLAS: How come there were more catalogues than money mail?

MS. BROWN: That puzzles you?

JASON: I think it's because there are more bills in this world, with taxes and stuff.

MS. BROWN: How many of you are standing in the category that matches your initial prediction? Eight out of the twenty-five students in the class predicted the exact category.

LIBBY: Something puzzles me. How come there is only one person that has received a friendly letter?

SADE: Fewer people received letters.

BRIAN: I know why we only have one, because most friends and family don't write, they use the telephone.

MS. BROWN: Do you think if we did this activity at another point in the year that we would get the same results?

TYLER: People might go on a shopping spree at the holidays and go nuts with their credit cards. That would make a lot of bills.

LIBBY: If you did this at Christmas, you would get more letters from friends and family too.

The next day the children revisited the data with a new task in hand. Random teams of four were formed to compile, organize, and make statements about their data. First, the students wrote down the number of pieces of mail for each category and combined their data to identify the grand total for their team. Then, each group was given a strip of cash register tape approximately one meter in length. Using a model developed by Charles Lovitt and Doug Clarke from Australia (1988, 143), the students used a ruler to mark the strip in centimeter intervals along the top of the paper up to the number of the grand total they calculated. To show the amounts in each category, the team started at the left edge and counted the total number in one of the groupings. At that point they made a line from the top of the strip to the bottom. For example, in the space to the left of that line, which represented the number of advertisements they had received, they wrote the word *Advertisements* in large letters and the actual subtotal underneath. From the line that marked the end of the advertisements section, the students counted the number of *Catalogues* and so on until the strip displayed the full complement of data. Then the teams wrote statements about what they noticed about the information they collected. Each group was to have enough statements so that all group members would be prepared to share. We noticed that the teams folded their strips to make comparisons using the segments rather than using the numerical counts. Also many students stood up when examining the strip, probably to gain perspective on the entire view of the proportions and relationships they were trying to find. One group stated "We had twice as much Money mail as we had Information mail." Another group found by folding that if they added their Advertisements, Letters, Money, and Information mail together that proportion almost equaled their Catalogue mail. One team concluded that their Money mail was about one-fourth of their total.

To look at the data in another way the students could take the strip of paper and cut on each of the lines. Using a stable baseline and the sections of the cash register tape a quick bar graph could be created. We tried another configuration. The students took the cash register tape and matching the beginning of the first category on the strip to the end of the last category, they attached the pieces with tape and formed a loop. Each team placed the loop on a large sheet of chart paper, and with a team member supporting the sides of the loop in place, another student traced the inside to create a circle. When they completed the circle, students drew marks around the circumference at the points where the categories changed. In other words where the full lines were indicated on the side of the strip graph, the students marked those places on the circle drawn on the chart paper. Using a straightedge, the teams connected the lines on the circumference to a point marked at the center of the circle. Then they labeled the five sections. This process enabled the students to quickly reorganize the data from a strip graph into a circle graph (see Figure 6–5).

Some students were surprised by how easy it was to see the size of the catalogues section on their circle graph as being greater than half. Although they knew that by statements they had already made, the visual evidence of the circle graph was more immediate.

A necklace made from one hundred beads was distributed to each group with the instructions to place the necklace around the center of the circle—in an equal distance from the midpoint, even if it did not align with the outside edge of the graph. If the necklace was on the edge or within the circle, they were ready for the next investigation. If the necklace made a wider concentric circle, then students were asked to use the straightedge to continue the lines distinguishing the different categories of mail out to meet the necklace. The students explored the values that they would get from counting how many beads were between the lines of each category.

At first many counted the beads in a category and just recorded the results, but when they reached the amount for the catalogue category they quickly counted all the beads on the necklace. When they realized there were one hundred beads, the volume of conversations increased as the connection to percent was made. The bead counting gave the students an informal approach to estimating percent and a solid and meaningful model of the per one hundred concept. One child was interested to know if the necklace could be used with the human circle graph the class had made the day before. She answered her own question as we retrieved the bicycle sprocket and tested how the necklace could be a tool in finding percentages in that circumstance.

The following class period the students walked around and viewed graphs made

Figure 6–5   *Paper loop diagram of circle graph*

by other teams. Then they analyzed the class data and hypothesized about why the results turned out this way. We put the question "What do you know?" on the board, then walked around with a pocket full of markers and a pad of paper. As students shared an idea, we asked them to write it down and tape it to the board. The following is part of the dialogue that accompanied the brainstorming:

MS. BROWN: I would like to move beyond giving numbered data. Explain your thinking.

COURTNEY: More people talk through computers or phones than letters. Only three out of seventy-six children in the three classes got letters that week.

SADE: At our house the bills come at different times a month.

MS. BROWN: Tell me about that.

SADE: The week that we counted the mail I received more bills, but the next week, I just watched and we did not get as many.

JESSICA: Maybe some people forgot to pay and they got more than one notice.

MICHAEL: I want to add to what Brian said. Since my house is up for sale, the Re-altor puts out flyers and mail letters to get people to buy the houses. He needs to get the message out. More companies send out flyers because it is cheaper than TV commercials.

RACHEL: The reason people got a lot of catalogues is because people might be looking for summer bargains.

TADD: I think they are getting a lot of catalogues because people buy more in the summer.

DEVIN: If we collected mail for an extended period of time, we would get more pieces of mail and have a better sample of what we really get more of.

As the discussion concluded, we reviewed what had been shared and then asked the students to write a hypothesis about the mail results.

Student Samples

Our discussions about the data provided information about where some of the students were in analyzing and evaluating data. This activity incorporated several concepts and gave a practical application for converting fractional parts to decimals. We could see the value of repeating this activity over the course of the year and looking for other categories to compare. Making a class chart during the analysis of the data involves more students, and by having them write their idea and share it, they pay closer attention to detail. The written data also gives students a jump-start when they begin writing about the mathematics. They have a reference point. You can more easily identify the students who are thinking deeply.

We posted the circle graphs on the wall and as a group made a statement about their graph, other students had to decide which graph was being discussed. Each team also tried to find a graph that appeared to be most similar to their data. This was an interesting task as some based their decision on a match in rank order, others based it on the size of the largest segment of the circle, and others still on a numerical match on a particular category, thereby missing the proportional nature of the comparison.

In response to the same story, another teacher in our school gave her class a piece of cash register tape and asked them to record for a week how deep the pile of mail received at home each day was. They used the actual cash register tape to mark the height and label it with the corresponding day. Students in the class had fun looking for trends in heavy mail days and light mail days for the neighborhood.

Higher-level problem solving can only occur when students are given multiple tasks that challenge them to explore new or different strategies to find solutions. These opportunities should allow for student talk, use of manipulatives, rethinking strategies, and sharing ideas. Girls need to practice self-assessment as they problem solve. Learning to examine their own thinking will enable them to identify when another strategy is needed to verify their first approach or to practice using an unfamiliar method. A variety of literature can be used to create problem-solving tasks that challenge students and encourage inventive thinking.

Works Cited

BURKE, CAROLYN. 1995. Conversation with Phyllis Whitin and David Whitin, 10 April.

DWECK, CAROL S., WILLIAM DAVIDSON, SHARON NELSON, and BRADLEY ENNA. 1978. "Sex Differences in Learned Helplessness: II. The Contingencies of Evaluative Feedback in the Classroom and III. An Experimental Analysis." *Developmental Psychology* 14: 268–76.

FENNEMA, ELIZABETH, and PENELOPE PETERSON. 1985. "Autonomous Learning Behavior: A Possible Explanation of Gender-related Differences in Mathematics." In *Gender Influences in Classroom Interaction*, edited by Louise Cherry Wilkinson and Cora B. Marrett, 17–35. New York: Academic Press.

KOEHLER, MARGARET S. 1990. "Classrooms, Teachers, and Gender Differences in Mathematics." In *Mathematics and Gender*, edited by Elizabeth Fennema and Gilah Leder, 128–46. New York: Teachers College Press.

LEDER, GILAH. 1990. "Teacher/Student Interactions in the Mathematics Classroom: A Different Perspective." In *Mathematics and Gender*, edited by Elizabeth Fennema and Gilah Leder, 149–68. New York: Teachers College Press.

LOVITT, CHARLES, and DOUG CLARKE. 1988. *The Mathematics Curriculum and Teaching Program: Activity Bank Number One*. Canberra, Australia: Curriculum Development Centre.

NATIONAL COUNCIL OF TEACHERS OF MATHEMATICS. 1989. *Curriculum and Evaluation Standards for School Mathematics*. Reston, VA: NCTM.

NATIONAL ACADEMY OF SCIENCES. 1989. *Everybody Counts: A Report to the Nation of the Future of Mathematics Education*. Washington, DC: National Academy Press.

VAN DE WALLE, JOHN. 1997. Blur the Line Between Performance Assessment and Instruction. Presentation given at the Annual Conference of the National Council of Teachers of Mathematics, Minneapolis, MN, 19 April.

Children's Literature

JACKSON, ELLEN. 1994. *Cinder Edna*. New York: Lothrop, Lee & Shepard Books.

MCDONALD, MEGAN. 1995. *Insects Are My Life*. New York: Orchard Books.

SPURR, ELIZABETH. 1996. *The Long, Long Letter*. New York: Hyperion.

STEVENS, KATHLEEN. 1994. *Aunt Skilly and the Stranger*. New York: Ticknor & Fields.

7

Connecting Mathematics to Life

In *Women's Ways of Knowing*, Belenky et al. (1986) emphasize the potency of connections in learning. They suggest that linking topics and lives are prerequisites for the most efficient learning of abstractions. Mathematics is infinitely richer when it is not divorced from other subject areas and when it is authentically linked to the real world. This artistic process of integrating mathematics across disciplines and into everyday life is the work of a teacher-artisan.

Connected Curriculum

In essence, this is the connected curriculum—connected teaching for the connected learner—that we aspire to. Mathematics is a human endeavor carried out by people, not by calculators or computers. When building a connected curriculum that honors the learning style of females, the key is to bridge manageable pieces of content to the life stories of others or to the students' experiences. This is where the "hearts-on" curriculum emerges. The learning is personalized through examining lives of great women in mathematics. The interactions between these leaders' thoughts and the very mathematics in which students are engaged make the kinds of links that build retention of information. A book such as *Celebrating Women in Mathematics and Science* (1996), edited by Miriam Cooney, is a fine place to begin. The key for connected learners is integrating thought, experience, and feeling by mathematics instruction that blurs the lines among these elements.

Linking the real world through applications and realistic settings and scenarios also provides insights to the purpose of studying the mathematics, encourages active use rather than passive retrieval of information, honors the students' existing knowledge, and helps students construct knowledge rather than encouraging mechanical use of facts and skills.

Letting students take leadership in the direction of the investigation acknowledges the students' connection and contribution to the curriculum. Such an inclusive model allows for choice and provides students with the opportunity to find a common thread while learning how to learn. Passionate learners can target the areas that draw their attention as they blend the various conceptual ingredients together.

Students can fully express their depth of understanding when they can capture the essence of a variety of ideas and link them meaningfully. As we encourage students to assimilate these broader connections, we are really preparing students for a complete application of the information. The venture thus becomes holistic.

Many attempts to integrate mathematics into a unit of study become nothing more than using a ruler to make a measurement or, even more artificially, collecting data on everything. Some activities developed in the name of integration are counterproductive. These instructional events link very easy and trivial mathematical concepts with a more complex social studies unit and suggest that mathematics has been taught. We highlight a different approach. Our integration process starts with a significant mathematics theme and moves outward in a search of significant work in related disciplines. If we believe our linkages are becoming artificial or we consider them developmentally "lightweight" we reevaluate the need for integration.

Helping students find the relationships and patterns between a mathematical concept and a story in a book, a bit of history, or a butterfly on the window requires movement among metaphors, analogies, conclusions, insights, and applications, which is very thought-provoking and stimulating.

Geo-Dolls

When we were scanning bookstores pursuing interesting tales of hardy female characters, we noticed that several of our favorite characters were available as cloth dolls. Deciding that these dolls might add to the reading of a story, we purchased one. After seeing the students' enthusiasm we purchased more dolls and as a result became involved in an exciting experience. We developed an idea to send the dolls with friends to places around the world and on interesting summer adventures. Locked in a zip-top plastic bag with a disposable camera and a journal, the dolls trekked around the globe to the Greenwich Date Line, tested water with a scientist on a white-water rafting expedition in Colorado, and attended the Atlanta Summer Olympics. We traced their journeys and asked their escorts to photograph the dolls in mathematical situations. The guardians were more than obliging. Many of the dolls became the highlight of their companions' tours. More important, everyone was thinking mathematically—and out of school! Some of the activities we describe are from the adventures of our band of traveling dolls.

Falling Bodies

This lesson was part of a series we did that explored geometry, gravity, and Galileo's Law of Falling Bodies. The literature became the vehicle for the activity and gave us another model of a young problem solver.

Bravo Tanya, a book written by Patricia Lee Gauch, tells us about tiny Tanya and her passion for dancing. Tanya and her ballerina bear, Barbara, dance "anywhere, anytime." When Tanya enters formal dance class she already knows ballet's ordinal positions by heart. But soon after, she experiences difficulty keeping in step when the piano is playing and the instructor is clapping and counting the beat. She continues attending class and has many frustrating mishaps. After a recital, Tanya overhears the instructor telling her mom, "Not everyone is a dancer." Tanya takes Barbara to their favorite spot by the brook. The ballerina bear wants to dance so Tanya dances with her to the music of the wind. The piano player from the dance class happens upon the two and claps and cheers, "Bravo!" Tanya and the piano player share their love of sounds and rhythms found in nature. The next week at dance class, when the instructor begins clapping and counting, Tanya just listens to the piano and hears a storm, ocean waves, and blowing branches in the wind and spins gracefully around the floor. As she departs from class, Tanya and the piano accompanist smile at each other, acknowledging their shared secret.

The book and Tanya's love of dance presented us with several options mathematically and scientifically. After the first reading, the students discussed the math wisdom and the message of the story. The discussion centered on not giving up and believing in yourself:

> COREY: If someone tells you that you are not doing very good, you can show them that you can do it.
> DANNY: If you believe in yourself you can accomplish a lot.
> JAMIE: It is not a good idea to quit. You should keep on trying.
> AMBER: You don't have to be what others want you to be.
> MS. BROWN: Where do you think we can find mathematics in this story? What do professional dancers do that might have a mathematical connection?
> ASHLEY: They have to follow patterns and repeat steps in their routines.
> BEN: The dancers have to follow a beat and stay in rhythm.
> MS. BROWN: What do people like about watching dancers?
> LAUREN: They like to watch dancers jump and be caught by another dancer or spin.
> ALISHA: Most dancers are not really heavy, so they are able to jump high.

Next, the students were given a pattern with a figure of a dancer. They had to follow the directions and construct a model (see Figure 7–1). The students completed their model construction and were given time to experiment and observe what the dancer could do. They found that, like a helicopter's whirling blades, this paper version of dancing Tanya could spin in the air at great speed.

Several students tried positioning paper clips in different places on the model. They also tested other variables such as dropping the model from different heights. During this exploratory time students discussed in small groups ideas about rotating and revolving, and how those concepts related to the model. Then the students were

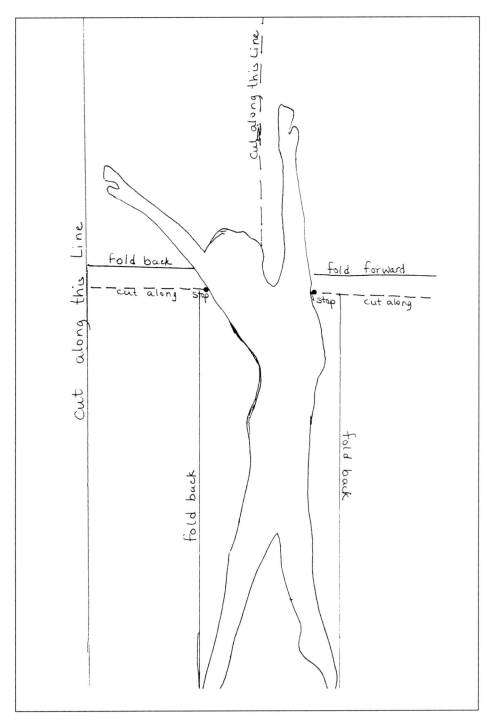

FIGURE 7–1   Tanya *pattern*

asked to hypothesize about the number of rotations the dancing model made before it touched the floor. The students made predictions and then worked in pairs to count the rotations. Several strategies were used during this phase, including putting pencil marks on the extended arms to aid in the counting process. Others tried sitting on the floor in a stationary position, while their partners dropped the model. Most groups agreed that it was not easy to accurately count the number of rotations.

Students climbed a ladder in the classroom and dropped their dancers from a height of eight feet. Other classmates timed the event and counted the number of full rotations. These data were recorded on a chart, and students looked for patterns in the number of rotations in the time it took to fall. They found no consistent pattern in the data to help them draw a firm conclusion. The students suspected that some classmates might have applied force, rather than just dropping their model, causing the results to vary. Ashley also wondered if the air conditioning coming on and going off would change the results.

At the next class session we used a "What Do You Know?" chart for the students to record their observations about the dancing model, Galileo's law, how the shape affects the speed of rotations, and what happened when they added paper clips. The question was then asked, "How many rotations will the model make when dropped from five feet?" They used their observations from the previous day and their background knowledge to develop and record their hypotheses.

Then, the teacher darkened the room and turned on a strobe light, which made the dancing figure appear as if it is in slow motion. (**Caution:** Please note that children with epilepsy or other central nervous system disorders should not view a strobe light.) Students were fascinated by the way the flash of the strobe light made what had been a difficult task of counting spins quite simple. Students were then provided ample time to explore their model, gather data, and record their observations. The children were reminded that scientists and mathematicians must repeat their experiments to validate their findings. In sharing their results, students felt it was easier to count the rotations with a strobe light. The final step for the students was to take the data they had collected, write conclusions, and analyze their experiences. Ashley writes:

> I found out that with the strobe light my hypothesis was correct. Tanya made five rotations in five feet. With the strobe light it makes everything look slower, because the light flashes and when it is off you can't see what is going on, but you see when it comes back on. That makes it easier to count.

Jessica writes:

> My ballet person rotated five times from five feet. It was easier to count the rotations when we used a strobe light. I can conclude that your eyes and light can play tricks on you. I know this because the strobe light didn't make the model turn slower it just appeared that way.

Brandon writes:

I found my hypothesis right and wrong because when I got close to the strobe light we used, I only counted four rotations, but as I got five feet away then it rotated five times, and when I moved back another five feet it rotated six. I'm not sure why my movement affected the turns. I need to do another experiment.

Through this task the students collected data, organized the information, and found measures of central tendency either by tallying a mode or calculating a mean. The data from a five-foot height was not conclusive for students to develop a hypothesis about one rotation for each foot of height. Experimenting at higher heights does present some hazards, but students continue to brainstorm future experiments that blend our scientific and mathematical skills.

The Strength of an Oak

Pearl Moscowitz's Last Stand, by Arthur Levine, tells the tale of a peaceful firebrand who, after living in a neighborhood her whole life, begins to witness changes that she cannot tolerate. Fortunately, Pearl inherits many good things from her mother, including her ability to problem solve with style and finesse. She tackles this particular situation with reasoned reflection and comes up with a dramatic solution.

In a related book, *Maxine's Tree*, by Diane Leger, Maxine is a younger problem solver, resisting change in another neighborhood. Like Pearl, she also uses logical thinking to come up with a solution. The setting of *Maxine's Tree* is a rain forest in British Columbia, Canada. Maxine and her family regularly visit a redwood forest where she homes in on her very favorite tree during each stopover. There she crawls under the huge trunk and revels in the glory of the tree's beauty. When her father brings her to an area that has been clear-cut for lumber, Maxine's concern for her treasured redwood is unmistakable. After considering the situation she states, "No one will want to hurt someone's favorite tree." So, she decides to name her tree. Marking a piece of wood with "Maxine's Tree" she hangs this identification on a limb. On the next visit she rushes to inspect her tree and finds names, sometimes in foreign languages, labeling many of the other trees in the forest. These books stimulated real-world applications and data collection.

In discussions of the tree stories, we focused on the strategies the characters used to find solutions. After reading *Pearl Moscowitz's Last Stand*, the students generated many ideas.

ERIC: Pearl said she would chain herself to the tree. Then all these newspeople and the mayor came to the tree. She called attention to herself and the tree.
MS. BROWN: What can you conclude about Pearl's problem solving?
CHRIS: She never gives up.
TYLER: She has lots of different strategies. She used logical reasoning when she stalled the guy and distracted him.

These stories were of particular interest to children in our school. In 1995, the school sponsored and planted the Stan LeMaster legacy tree museum on the school grounds. The sixty-five trees represent a living tribute to great people, such as the Joan-of-Arc Willow, Sir Isaac Newton Apple, Laura Ingalls Cottonwood, and the Amelia Earhart Maple. Taken from cuttings gathered from trees all over the world by an amateur horticulturist, the saplings were planted and are now tended in a quarter-mile walking track around the school. This outdoor science classroom has been an endless resource for linking mathematics, science, and history.

Linking the stories to our botanical collection brought out many ideas:

MS. BROWN: How do the trees in our legacy tree museum compare and contrast with Maxine's tree?

JOHN: Ours are much smaller, because they have only been planted there for just two years.

LAUREN: It takes thousands of years to grow a tree like Maxine's.

BRIAN: The piece of wisdom I got from this book is that if you can start something, like Maxine did, someone else could add on to it.

That was just exactly what we were going to do! The class proceeded to collect some numbered data on the trees in the Stan LeMaster tree museum by using mathematical and scientific skills. The students decided to preserve an ongoing record of the growth of these special trees. To establish the tradition of monitoring and recording their growth rate we asked a series of questions:

What do you see as important information that would document the growth process of trees?

What would be a mathematical way to record the data so that it would be easy to interpret?

How will we display these data for future classes so they can continue charting the growth?

What mathematical tools would assist us with this investigation?

We asked the students to be like Pearl and Maxine and for each to select a single tree for data collection. We discussed the importance of collecting the same information so the data could be accurately and meaningfully recorded. Here are some thoughts children had about information that should be gathered:

ASHLEY: Record the height of the tree.

KATIE: The number of branches on the tree.

AMBER: The width of the tree.

MS. BROWN: How would we measure the width of a tree?

DAVID: Isn't the circumference divided by three equal to the diameter?

MS. BROWN: Maybe what we need is to measure the circumference then too. How are we going to organize these data for future classes?

JESSICA: It would be easy to add data to a spreadsheet each year.

MS. BROWN: What mathematical tools could we use to measure the different properties of the tree?

BRANDON: A tape measure to measure height and width.

SARA: Meter- or yardsticks to measure the trees' height.

MS. BROWN: In order to make the data consistent from year to year we must decide on a unit of measurement. What should we use?

SARA: Centimeters. Maybe people in the future won't be using inches.

We reviewed the process to find circumference and several methods to find a tree's height. Students practiced by measuring someone's wrist or another cylindrical object in the room. In measuring an item taller than themselves, we discussed that students could use a novel but quite accurate method. You can approximate the height of a tall tree by walking far enough away from the tree so that (with your back to the tree) you can just see the top of the tree when you bend over and look through your legs. Then using trundle wheels, you measure from that point back to the base of the tree. That distance is an approximation of the tree's height. The activity proceeded and the students went out to collect data. We encouraged students to support each other and validate their measurements. Because most of the trees were seedlings, the students did not need to use the trundle wheel or clinometer methods to determine the trees' height.

After several days of collecting and recording new data, the class viewed our spreadsheets and discussed what was found. They compared these measurements to those they had taken from September and to those collected by another group from the May before.

MS. BROWN: Let's take some time to analyze the data and state what we can conclude about our tree museum.

LOGAN: I think they are growing, because at first measure we didn't even think the Andrew Jackson Magnolia was there. But now it is twenty-five centimeters tall.

MARAT: When you look at the numbers, it looks like some trees have shrunk. I think some of them have been damaged.

SADE: All of the trees I measured were less than fifteen centimeters in circumference.

MICHAEL: I could tell that the ones I measured were young trees, because the circumference was less than five centimeters.

MS. BROWN: How does the circumference give you information about the age of the tree?

MICHAEL: Older trees are wider and you can hide behind them, some you can't get your hands around. With all of these trees you could put your hand around the trunk.

JESSICA: We have a variety of heights in our tree data.

MATTHEW: I know that most of the trees are between ninety centimeters and two meters in height.

MS. BROWN: What puzzled you about this collection of data?

SADE: How could trees from other countries, like Germany, that have different climates, grow here in Louisville, Kentucky?

SARA: Could Maxine's sequoia survive in our tree museum?

MS. BROWN: That is an interesting question. Mr. LeMaster, the designer of this tree museum, is a horticulturist, and he selected the trees. He must have done research about the tree and its ability to grow in Kentucky. Does anything else puzzle you?

MARAT: How did those trees shrink?

MS. BROWN: Let's talk about that. Do you think they actually shrunk?

SADE: I don't think they shrunk, I think the people who measured them in September may not have measured correctly.

LAUREN: I wonder what the average height and circumference would be.

MS. BROWN: We could find that out mathematically. What patterns did you see?

KATRINA: I think I saw a pattern in the way they were planted. Big, medium, small, big, medium, small.

MS. BROWN: What kind of evidence does the chart provide?

JOHN: Over half of the trees are growing. Our chart shows the trees have grown three or four centimeters in height since they were measured last May.

SARA: We should keep working on our measuring skills to make sure we are getting accurate numbers for our chart.

MARAT: We need to take better care of our trees. Some of the data on the chart makes it look like some trees are not growing. I think we need to give them fertilizer.

MS. BROWN: One of the purposes of this project is to instill pride in the history we have growing on our school grounds. I want you to write your thoughts and reflections on this project (see Figure 7–2).

Our mathematics classes have begun their own legacy of recording growth and looking for patterns. We will continue to make connections between mathematics, science, and history through our tree museum and the examples set by Pearl and Maxine. Another book that complements the discussions of old trees, particularly redwoods, is *The Ever-Living Tree* by Linda Vieira. Through a time line that traces historical events during various points in the tree's development, wonderful ties between several subjects can be made.

How Does Your Garden Grow?

Inspirations: Stories About Women Artists by Leslie Sills is an enlightening book about the lives of four females who have made major contributions to the art world: Georgia

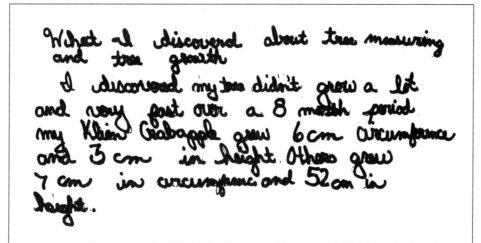

FIGURE 7–2   *Sade's analysis of the tree measuring project*

O'Keeffe, Frida Kahlo, Alice Neel, and children's book author and illustrator Faith Ringgold. We chose to read to the children the profile of the artist Georgia O'Keeffe.

From the age of thirteen, Georgia's goal was set on making painting her life. Although she faced strong feedback from teachers, she maintained confidence and persisted.

What became important to Georgia was nature, patterns, abstractions, and "filling space in beautiful ways." Not surprising in the 1920s, lush depictions of flowers became one of her most favorite subjects. Georgia stated, "I'll paint what I see—what the flower is to me, but I'll paint it big and they will be surprised into taking time to look at it—I will make even busy New Yorkers take time to see what I see of flowers" (Sills 1989, 14).

Since many of these floral oil paintings are over three feet wide and four feet long, the size and detail of the flowers fascinated the children. To assist the children in understanding something about the enlarging process we engaged them in several mathematical activities.

First we found a large picture of a hollyhock covered with dewdrops. Using a color copying machine we enlarged it to the size of an eight-inch-by-ten-inch piece of paper. We marked the print with a grid composed of two-inch-by-two-inch squares. On the back of the print, the squares were numbered in consecutive order and then were cut out along the lines. Each child was given a two-inch-by-two inch square and a blank eight-inch-by-eight-inch piece of white paper. We discussed how we could enlarge the design on the little square. The children suggested that if they worked on one part of their grid square at a time then they could visualize the image better on the larger paper. That process seemed to make sense. By duplicating each line, contour, and color, they drew a seemingly abstract picture. On a bulletin board we fashioned a frame that measured thirty-two inches by forty inches. As children finished their facsimiles, they mounted their enlarged image on the corresponding spot. At first the "flower" did not appear to look very similar to O'Keeffe's, but as more pieces were mounted, it became easier to recognize the original colorful hollyhock. Even though some shadings were lighter or darker than others, the students were amazed at what they had accomplished.

Then the class started to discuss the mathematics. How much bigger was our "Georgia O'Keeffe" flower than the one used as an initial model? At first the students made arguments that the new representation was four times as large. They described the sides of the small square they were given as being two inches in length and the large square as eight inches in length, thus leading them to the conclusion that it was four times larger. We asked them to carry that thinking when they considered the dimensions of the original flower and the one on the bulletin board. Again this seemed to make sense. The hollyhock model was eight inches by ten inches and the enlargement was thirty-two inches by forty inches, which is four times greater. Then we used some black-and-white (eight-inch-by-ten-inch) copies of the original hollyhock and gave a student four of them, stating, "Since the big flower is four times as large, cover the huge flower with these copies of the four original flowers." One child tacked up the papers on the left edge of the painting leaving the rest of flower uncovered and the other students speechless.

Most were quite confused. What had seemed a logical and well-reasoned conclusion clearly did not work. We asked students to talk with each other and think about two things: How much of the large flower was covered with the four original pieces? And how many more pictures of the original size would they need to cover the whole flower? Immediately the students set to work. Since the child who had placed the four pictures of the original O'Keeffe flower on the bulletin board tacked them down in a vertical column, some students took them off and reconfigured their placement. They wanted to place the photocopies in a square in the upper left-hand corner. One child reported, "Now I see it, only one-fourth of the large flower is covered." Other pairs of students used additional copies of the original flower to test exactly how many would be needed. They experimented and found that it would take precisely sixteen. Although most students had solved it visually, we needed to go back to the mathematics concepts. We asked the students, What mathematics concept was involved when we wanted to talk about covering something? Several students were able to connect it to measuring area. When given that clue, teams started discussing the possibilities. Area worked! They found the dimensions finally fit this new model in their head. Jessica remarked, "It is four times larger in both directions (length and width). That's why it is sixteen times bigger." The visual experimentation enabled the students to bridge what they knew to what they didn't know.

In another activity we used reproductions of O'Keeffe's *Petunias, Morning Glories, Orchid, Irises, Oriental Poppies,* and *Lilies* to make our own artful garden. Using a method called the "stretcher," students created proportional enlargements. The stretching activity uses heavy-duty rubber bands that are approximately three inches in length. On the chalkboard we demonstrated a way to copy figures using the bands. Using two rubber bands slipknotted together in a fairly tight knot, we drew a small square on the chalkboard. Securing one band loop with a finger down in a corner below and to the left of the square and having a piece of chalk in the opposite end you trace the drawing of the square with the knot. In other words, the knot follows the contours of the figure while the chalk held by the taut rubber band draws an enlarged reproduction. The students were given a centimeter grid paper with a four-by-four square and were asked to experiment. Holding the band they followed the edges of the original drawing and re-created the small square—but in an enlarged version. You could hear the oohs and aahs. Some of the students found it difficult to keep the finger in the stationary loop position from moving. They had to practice to maintain the exact location throughout the tracing.

> Ms. ALLEN: What did you notice about the second square?
>
> ALI: The square is a lot bigger.
>
> Ms. ALLEN: How could you compare the two squares mathematically?
>
> NINA: There are sixteen square units in the little one because it's a four-by-four square. There are about sixty-six units in the big square. It's about eight-by-eight and a little. Some of the edges are not even.
>
> Ms. ALLEN: Thinking back to our flower painting, how many little squares would it take to cover your enlarged square?
>
> ALI: I think four. It's two times larger on one side and two times larger on the other.

The connections we made between the two projects helped students see the problem as one of area, not just linear increase. Once students had explored the potential of the stretchers, they used the them to copy O'Keeffe's flowers. Through experimentation with the rubber bands, students found two rubber bands knotted together would double the dimensions and thereby quadruple the area, and three rubber bands knotted together would triple the dimensions and create an area nine times the original size. They decided on the size they wanted and created exciting images of the flowers. When they finished, they wrote about the mathematics in their drawing. Then we used a digital camera to take photos of their work and embed the pictures into their mathematical writings on the computer.

Finding links between mathematics and art can bring many new students into the mix. This blending can greatly help children who are visual learners by using their spatial strengths in thinking proportionally.

Global Gadfly

Nellie Bly's Monkey is a story of an adventurous female reporter's trip around the world. The author tells the story from the point of view of the reporter's monkey,

McGinty. McGinty writes about Miss Bly's courage and strength. When the class completed the story of Nellie's journey, we started our discussion with what the challenges would be in circumnavigating the globe in 1890. The students' conversation proceeded in this way:

MS. BROWN: What kind of mathematical ideas could we gather from this book?

STEVIE: Maybe about how many days it took to travel around the world.

MS. BROWN: Is it reasonable to think that Nellie could travel around the world in seventy-two days?

STEPHANIE: Yes, because this book tells about a real event, so it really did happen.

JOSIE: The book showed the day she left and the day she arrived, so it really is seventy-two days.

ASHLEE: She broke a record.

MS. BROWN: What does she mean in the book when she states that she is racing with time alone?

BRIAN: I think she is trying to see how fast she could make it around the world, set her own record. I don't think she was really racing against someone else.

GEORGE: I thought of another math idea. She had to pay for that monkey and probably couldn't use USA money.

NICHOLAS: It said that she had to pay with seven coins. I wonder what they would be worth.

CAITLIN: She had to follow a schedule, because it said her train came in at 9:40.

MICHAEL: She had to figure out how much time to spend in each country.

JASON: She had to plot a course around the world on a map.

MS. BROWN: What do you think was involved with a trip of this magnitude in 1889?

BRANDON: They had to go by train or boat. There were no other choices.

SADE: It took her fifteen days on the boat to get back to the USA.

JOHN: I think the moral of the story is that when you have brains you can do anything you want if you just try hard.

MS. BROWN: I want you to study this map of her route. We are going to do some activities with direction and compasses. [At this point I held up the transparent circular protractor-compass (Figure 7–3).] These are not navigational compasses with a magnet. These transparent models with the string attached to the center will be used as a directional guide.

We planned an activity for a multiage classroom of fourth- and fifth-grade students that would reinforce their knowledge of cardinal directions and map reading. The students were furnished with a map of the continental United States, the transparent directional compass, and strips of paper. Globes were also available. The students were instructed to write trip itineraries: for example, "I traveled from Indianapolis, Indiana, to Seattle, Washington" or "I am going to Las Vegas, Nevada,

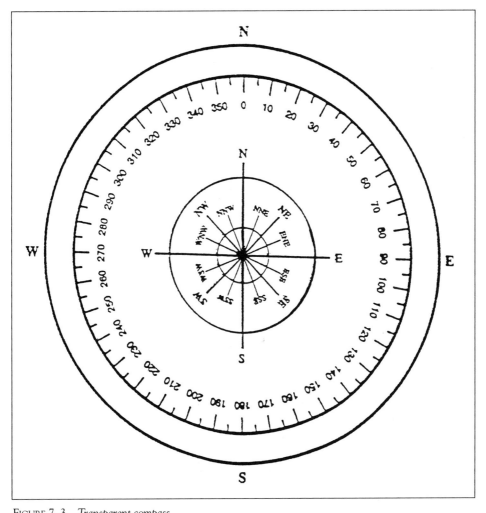

FIGURE 7–3   *Transparent compass*

from Louisville, Kentucky." The students worked cooperatively, and we circulated, reading their travel statements. The remainder of that class period students practiced with the transparent compasses. They needed to make sure that they held the compass with the north and south true to the map's compass rose. Then we would call out a city and state and they would have to identify its cardinal direction from Louisville, Kentucky.

The following day, students were anxious to begin their Compass Point activity. A chart was made with a list of the cardinal directions. The students were divided into eight teams and each team was named for a direction: North, South, East, West, Northeast, Northwest, Southeast, Southwest. A travel statement from the student itineraries made the previous day was drawn out of a box, and teams determined the bearing in degrees needed to travel between one city and another using the transparent compasses. Traveling that involved polar routes was particularly challenging and intriguing. The students found that using a globe was necessary to accurately map out these routes.

To introduce coordinates we used a four-by-four-foot vinyl cloth with an x- and y-axis and a grid made from tape. We had the students stand and do a little coordinate geometry movement. This activity was a way to help the children remember to name the coordinate for the x-axis followed by the coordinate for the y-axis. We used spatial and kinesthetic cues and clues as often as we could. Our movement involved stepping to the east, stepping to the west, stepping to the north, and stepping to the south. After our steps, each student wrote their name on a sticky note; we placed one name on the grid and asked students to identify the note's position. We had a few guesses, and finally someone gave the (x, y) coordinates. Then the students talked about ways the coordinates could be written so people would always be able to follow the directions. Students then placed their names on different points on the grid. We worked through locating the first five with coordinate points as a group and then the students worked independently to record the remaining positions. After the work was complete, each student identified their coordinates and did a self-assessment.

The next phase of this lesson included an introduction to one of our traveling geo-dolls, *The Paper Bag Princess*, Elizabeth. This companion doll to Robert Munsch's story about a princess who is noted for her dragon-slaying ability traveled to England on a castle tour and returned with photographs from her journey. We presented Elizabeth in an "investigation center" so students could mathematically explore the distance of her journey, the dimensions of London Bridge, and the time it reads on Big Ben when our school day starts.

On one of Elizabeth's adventures, she visited the prime meridian. Her escort had captured the moment in a photograph of the doll standing on the official line of longitude. This connection became a motivating point of entry for examining the worldwide grid used to help navigate on the open seas and in the air. The activity we planned linked to the compass point lesson conducted the week before. This time instead of just directional words we added more numbered data with degrees of latitude and longitude. The class practiced reading the coordinates using both the degrees and the directional cue. They easily grasped the idea of the need for two coordinates from the previous work with grids. The type of map projection used clearly showed the grid lines and the numbers. By using maps that had a preprinted grid system, the less spatial learners could incorporate the coordinate system and have more access to success. Working with their groups, they again wrote travel statements, but this time they included the latitude and longitude.

We would revisit and discuss the real-world use of coordinates with navigation each time the students did this activity. Over the years we have taught latitude and longitude in varying ways. This time, the connections made among the mathematics, the feisty females in our stories, and the map work made the concept come alive.

For all types of learners, the sequence of moving from directional cues to coordinates, then to the use of directional and latitude and longitude degrees gave them greater opportunity for success. Having had a positive experience with this activity the students consistently ask to locate points on the map when the class considers locations of news stories. This activity, which incorporated geography, mathematics, and students' spatial intelligences, certainly left a lasting impression, and will be one we repeat in the future.

Cascading Cassie

Cassie Lightfoot is a delightful character from Faith Ringgold's *Tar Beach*. A tar beach is located on the rooftop of many apartment buildings in New York. Although there is nothing at this "beach" but laundry drying on clotheslines and heating machinery, families all over the city meet neighbors there, set up beach chairs and towels to bask in the sun, and picnic under the stars. Cassie particularly enjoys looking at the bridge from her perch on the top of her building.

Since Cassie is a part of our geo-doll collection, she recently traveled to Chicago, her hometown in New York City, and to the Summer Olympics in Atlanta. While at the Olympics, she attended the opening ceremonies, saw the U. S. women's basketball team play, watched the gymnasts, and saw swimmers and divers in competition.

When we read *Tar Beach* and learned that Cassie's fantasy gave her the ability to fly over city rooftops, the students thought of Cassie diving and flipping in the air, not unlike the Olympic gymnasts and divers. We used the idea of Cassie's imaginative flying to develop knowledge of geometric concepts such as rotation and flips in the context of diving. The doll became our model and performer in demonstrating dives.

We designed this activity for fourth-year and fifth-year mathematicians. The students would use a portion of their mathematics period working with Cassie. This was not an introductory lesson on rotation and flips. We had done skill work with attribute blocks and measuring angles earlier in the year, so this activity was building on prior knowledge. Because the doll has an irregular shape, we would never recommend this as a point of entry into the concepts of rotation and flips for younger students. We introduced Cassie to small groups during our investigation center time (see Figure 7–4). We reminded the students about her flying ability and reexamined the books *Tar Beach* as well as *Aunt Harriet and the Underground Railroad*. They were familiar with the "flying" characters and the stories. The students were given a sheet (see Figure 7–5) with a description of Cassie's eight diving maneuvers. We demonstrated what each of the eight maneuvers looked like using the doll.

Then students were given a paper model of Cassie to examine the vertical, horizontal, and diagonal axes. The vertical and horizontal flips were easier for them to visualize when we gave some clues. We told them that we could do a vertical flip, but

FIGURE 7–4   *Model of Cassie*

that they would have to call 911 if we attempted a horizontal flip. That image stuck with them, because we would hear the children working together and say, "Remember, Ms. Brown can't do a horizontal flip." Practicing the diagonal flips gave us a clear picture of the students that were not spatially oriented. We would put our hands over their hands and flip their models on the diagonal several times to give them a feel for the movement. We had to review many times how to determine if it was a left or right diagonal. We suggested placing the left hand in the upper left-hand corner and the right hand on the lower right to make a left diagonal flip. The reverse of this hand placement would be a right diagonal flip. Looking carefully at their hand placement helped the students self-correct.

To make a successful dive, Cassie must start **<u>standing up straight and facing forward.</u>**

When she lands in the water, she must be **<u>upside down and facing backward.</u>**

She always rotates **<u>counter-clockwise.</u>**

Cassie can perform eight tricks;

Trick	Symbol
Rotate 90°	90°
Rotate 180°	180°
Rotate 270°	270°
Rotate 360°	360°
Flip vertical	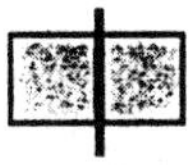
Flip horizontal	
Flip diagonal left	
Flip diagonal right	

FIGURE 7–5   *Cassie's eight moves*

We practiced making all eight maneuvers by asking a student in the small group to demonstrate a single move and asking the others to identify which maneuver was performed. Vocabulary was being practiced along with the movements. Then we gave students the data recording sheets (see Figure 7–6). Initially we wanted them to attempt to find and record more than one way to make a dive, and for many students this was overwhelming. The small group then started on attempting each maneuver one time, to see if they could get a successful dive. We stayed with them, and watched as they worked through the columns that reflected their first and second moves.

> MS. BROWN: Now I want you to start recording your data about all the successful dives that Cassie can make. If you cannot find a solution then put an x in that space. Let's begin with a 90-degree rotation in one move. Remember, Cassie can only move counterclockwise. What can we use as a visual reminder?
>
> BETH: We can use the second hand on the clock as a visual reminder, and always go the opposite way.
>
> MS. BROWN: If you move your Cassie model 90 degrees, in what direction will her head point?
>
> LOGAN: She looks like she is suspended in the air, lying on her left side.
>
> MS. BROWN: Can we find a way to move her 90 degrees and get a successful dive?
>
> JOHN: She can only roll to her left side, because she can't go clockwise.

The group then experimented with 180-degree, 270-degree, and 360-degree rotations.

> SARA: It would be impossible for a human being to do a 270-degree rotation, because they can't stop in the middle and hang in the air.
>
> MS. BROWN: Do Olympic divers have to do difficult moves to get higher scores?
>
> JESSICA: Oh, yes, they could do those tricks, because they are trained.
>
> MS. BROWN: Well, Cassie will give you the opportunity to train yourself on the meaning of rotations and flips.

The Cassie investigation center activity spanned two weeks. The students often worked in pairs and tested each other's ideas. The organization of the data sheets appeared to be more difficult than we had thought or intended. For example, in the 90-degree row, each dive from one to eight moves had to start with 90 degrees. We envisioned that the students would just add another move to the preceding dive, but they did not. Each time they began all over again, creating a different series of moves. We did see the students use repetitions as the activity began to get more challenging. The students really supported each other and willingly demonstrated moves to other groups. We would often hear a comment about a dive being impossible, and

Diving Cassie's Dazzling Day

Give two different solutions for each starting move if possible. When scoring, you receive one point for every successful dive and two points for each successful dive that does not repeat a move.

First Move ↓	in 1 move	in 2 moves	in 3 moves	in 4 moves	in 5 moves
Rotate 90°					
Rotate 180°					
Rotate 270°					
Rotate 360°					
Flip Vertical					
Flip Horizontal					
Flip Diagonal Left					
Flip Diagonal Right					

FIGURE 7–6   *Cassie recording sheet*

then someone would say, "Oh no it isn't. I found a way." Of course everyone loved to use the actual Cassie doll. They would hold on to her braids and left or right leg to make the diagonal flips.

Our closure for this activity included sharing ideas, posting them on a chart, and carrying out an open-ended assessment. We made a chart on the front board with the headings: "What do we know?," "What puzzles us?," "What patterns did we see?," and

"What strategies did we use?" First, we asked them to share their ideas about Cassie in the category, "What do you know?"

At this point the teachers had pockets full of markers and handfuls of paper strips. As students would share an idea, we would give out a piece of paper and a marker and ask them to write it down and tape it to the chart heading.

JESSICA: I know that Cassie can do four different flips: vertical, horizontal, left and right diagonal.

SCOTTY: She makes 90-, 180-, 270-, and 360-degree rotations.

ELIZABETH: She can only move counterclockwise.

DEREK: She gets two points for a dive if she doesn't repeat a move.

KENDRA: In order for Cassie to do a successful dive, she must face you when she starts, but be upside down and backward when she completes her dive.

SUSIE: There are many different ways of getting her in a correct diving position.

BRANDON: There is only one way with one move to get in the perfect diving position.

JESSICA: Cassie can't have a successful dive when she is facing you.

MS. BROWN: Some of you seemed puzzled when six, seven, and eight moves were needed. What puzzled you?

ASHLEE: It puzzled me that she could only do eight different moves.

ELIZABETH: When we started with a diagonal left or right it really tricked me.

LaGRACSHA: Is it possible to make eight moves without repeating a move once and have a successful dive?

COURTNEY: I got the diagonal left and diagonal right flips mixed up all the time.

MS. BROWN: Perhaps someone will be able to share a strategy with you.

JOHN: When I got up to five or more moves, I found it hard not to repeat a move twice in a row.

MS. BROWN: Let's move to the next heading, "What patterns did you see?" I want you to look and analyze your own data.

JASON: Almost every successful move had a rotation of 90 and 180 degrees.

ALEX: In all my four move columns, each dive has a 90-degree rotation in it.

DEVIN: On the vertical flip column all of my moves ended in a 360-degree move.

MATTHEW: In almost all of my moves I see that they ended with a rotation, not a flip.

MS. BROWN: Great observation, no one has stated that before.

ELIZABETH: In a lot of my moves my answers would be in a pattern of 360, 90, 360 degrees.

ROY: I have a 360-degree move in almost every dive.

BRANDI: In all of my dives I used a vertical flip.

JASON: In my 270-degree row, I noticed that all my moves started with a 270-degree rotation, then a diagonal left flip, and then the other moves.

MS. BROWN: Now that you have seen that pattern, can you figure out why that happened each time? Some of you who were more successful than others

Cassie and Mrs. Brown want to find out what you learned about flips and rotations. You may use drawings or pictures along with your written explanation for the problems below.

Please feel free to use the data you collected to help you with these problems.

1. Cassie wants to make (one dive) and do the (fewest movements) *Describe in words and show with pictures or diagrams* how she could make a successful dive.

To do one dive and with the fewest moves she would just do a horizontal flip to end up upside down and backwards.

2. In your investigation of rotations and flips what patterns did you discover...

The patterns that I discovered were: 1 almost all my rotate 270° went 270°(Diagonal left. 2. In my 180's I had a pattern between them ending in 180 and vertical flip.

3. Cassie wants to compete in a diving contest and she wants to be able to perform a challenging dive. *Describe in words and show with pictures or diagrams* the one you would recommend. (you may use the back of this sheet) *Why do you feel this is the most challenging dive?* A challenging dive would be, a /, then, rotate 90°, then, rotate another 360° — flip, and a \ flip.

FIGURE 7–7   *Elizabeth's assessment of Cassie's dives*

may have found some patterns to share. We would like you to help others who did not find those strategies.

REECE: When I got to seven and eight moves, I felt almost brain dead. I would use a 360-degree rotation. If you are in the diving position and you only need one more move to complete all the moves you can always rotate 360 degrees.

DEVIN: I did a lot of samples and tried them out.

TYLER: Sometimes I would reverse ones that I had tried.

MS. BROWN: Did anyone try just rearranging the moves?

MEGHAN: I did and sometimes it would work.

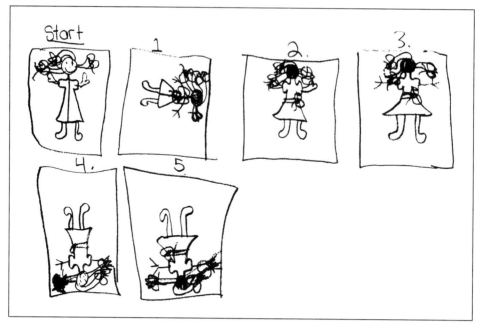

FIGURE 7–8   *Elizabeth's drawings of Cassie diving*

At this point in the lesson, the class had created a data bank and students were ready for the assessment (see Figures 7–7 and 7–8). We made sure that they understood that they needed to use their linguistic, mathematical, and spatial intelligences, and that just drawing a diagram or picture alone would not be enough. We made it clear that we were looking for a picture of *how they think*. Students were also told that the class's data bank might be valuable to some who were not able to see any patterns in their own data.

When the students had completed their assessments, we devoted a time to the Mathematician's Chair. This is where students take turns sharing mathematical writings or investigation with their peers, not unlike the popular Author's Chair for reading and listening to written compositions. Using this forum the students talked about their responses and had the class check their descriptions of dives for accuracy.

Ms. Brown: Stephanie is in the Mathematician's Chair to share her most challenging dive. The rest of you have the model of Cassie so you can try the dive she describes.

Stephanie: The most challenging dive that I have discovered is a seven-move dive. First rotate 180 degrees, second do a horizontal flip, third a diagonal left flip, fourth a diagonal right flip, fifth a 360-degree rotation, sixth a 270-degree rotation, and seventh a 90-degree rotation.

MS. BROWN: Stephanie, can you share with us why you think that is a challenging dive?

STEPHANIE: I think this is challenging because she does a lot of moves and does not repeat a move more than once.

MS. BROWN: Our next featured mathematician is Ben.

BEN: First I would make her do a vertical flip, then she would do a 360-degree rotation followed by a diagonal right flip. After that she would zip around in a horizontal flip. Then she would do a 90-degree rotation, then a 180-degree rotation. This is challenging because she does almost every possible move and she does not repeat any moves.

The Cassie activity provided rich insights into how children internalize the concepts of vertical, horizontal, and diagonal flips. While most students easily grasped the angles of the rotations, some children struggled even to the point of the assessment with the flips. In reflection, the chart could be divided into smaller increments and perhaps we could spend more time drawing diagrams to show what they are doing. Their confusion with vertical and horizontal puzzled us. Even with the paper model and straws attached to the side of the tagboard figure to represent the endpoints of the two axes, the students remained unsure. Perhaps more explorations with manipulatives and more applications of the meanings of vertical and horizontal in real-world settings would provide the mental model they needed. We also believe that starting with this activity earlier could have enabled students to build on these ideas throughout the year.

Conventional curriculum artificially divides life experience into compartments that have little connection with students' experience. In reality we live in a world where these lines are blurred. With Tanya, Pearl, Maxine, Nellie, Elizabeth, and Cassie we explored Galileo's theories, recorded data on the growth of trees, experimented with geometrical ideas, traveled around the world on paper and in our minds, and made artful connections with the work of Georgia O'Keeffe. The stories gave the students a realistic setting and purpose for their investigations. The link among science, geography, art, and mathematics can provide students and teachers with integrated, meaningful, and memorable lessons.

Works Cited

BELENKY, MARY, BLYTHE CLINCHY, NANCY GOLDBERGER, and JILL TARULE. 1986. *Women's Ways of Knowing: The Development of Self, Voice, and Mind.* New York: Basic Books.

COONEY, MIRIAM, ED . 1996. *Celebrating Women in Mathematics and Science.* Reston, VA: NCTM.

Children's Literature

BLOS, JOAN W. 1996. *Nellie Bly's Monkey.* New York: Morrow Junior Books.

GAUCH, PATRICIA LEE. 1992. *Bravo, Tanya.* New York: The Putnam & Grosset Group.

LEGER, DIANE. 1990. *Maxine's Tree*. Custer, WA: Orca Book Publishers.

LEVINE, ARTHUR. 1993. *Pearl Moscowitz's Last Stand*. New York: William Morrow and Company.

MUNSCH, ROBERT. 1980. *The Paper Bag Princess*. Toronto: Annick Press Ltd.

RINGGOLD, FAITH. 1991. *Tar Beach*. New York: Crown Publishers.

SILLS, LESLIE. 1989. *Inspirations: Stories About Women Artists*. Niles, IL: Albert Whitman & Company.

VIEIRA, LINDA. 1994. *The Ever-Living Tree: The Life and Times of a Coast Redwood*. New York: Walker & Co.

Concluding Thoughts

Where Are We Now?

Through examining studies on gender and experimenting in our classrooms, we have embarked on research that has changed the way we teach and encouraged our roles as mentors for females in all aspects of our lives. We have gone from being invisible and silent on many issues to developing strong voices in addressing our concerns. In the words of Dorney, we have begun to practice "habits of courage" (1995, 63).

Feisty Thoughts

Our habits of courage have emerged in different ways. Here are two stories of the changes that have taken place over the last two years. This is how Todd describes her transformation:

> Our Feisty Female action research has been a life-altering event professionally and personally. Initially, I participated in this project out of a heartfelt enjoyment of children's literature and an appetite for additional applications in mathematics. In the beginning, I spent countless hours reading and rereading books with strong females, searching for mathematical links. I must say I was guilty of thinking that if the mathematics was not obvious I could not use the story in a mathematics classroom.
>
> My breakthrough came with Anne Isaac's story, *Swamp Angel*. Here was a character that I loved, and as a result, felt compelled to find a connection so that I could use this tall tale in my mathematics class. As so often is the case, a child led the way. After reading the book to the children, a student said, "Angelica wasn't your average child." This comment brought on a revelation and a revolution. Lights went off in my head, ideas began to formulate, and the results are contained in the pages of this book. Literature opens doors to learning opportunities.
>
> Although the literature was the catalyst for our research, to effectively use the best strategies I had to focus on my instructional practices. I always believed that I

was striving to reach all students, but I had my share of quiet, nonparticipatory females in mathematics. Through reading literature on females' learning styles and dialogues with other interested colleagues, I put my teaching techniques under the microscope. I started to analyze the best ways to reach and teach girls.

Jessica came into my class as a very shy and reserved fourth grader. She was an excellent writer, but did not care for mathematics and did not have much self-confidence. As the year progressed, she heard stories about hardy females, and I nurtured her communication skills, and she began talking more in small groups. Still she was not comfortable speaking in front of the class. In the transition stage before Jessica was able to develop her own voice, she allowed me to read and share her reflections with the class. Jessica grasped ideas quickly, but liked working with manipulatives to help her act out the models she was trying to get into her head. She took the state mathematics assessment that year and scored the highest possible ranking, "Distinguished." Examining the results of that test, I noticed that our elementary school produced four distinguished student portfolios, three of which were from girls in my mathematics class.

Jessica returned to my mathematics classroom for a second year as a fifth grader, and as time progressed her confidence soared. I provided her with more opportunities to try new mathematics strategies and take risks. The trajectory of her mathematical growth was astounding. In addition, she eagerly took leadership roles in group activities and was comfortable sharing her mathematics writings in front of the class. She invested countless extra hours on her state-mandated mathematics portfolio and earned a "Proficient" score. Jessica's grandmother who was a volunteer in school stopped me in the hallway one day and said "I cannot believe the growth I have seen in Jessica. She is always talking about how she loves math."

I kept in touch with Jessica's school experiences through contact with her grandmother. She caught me in my classroom one morning, before my class arrived, to relate Jessica's latest breakthrough. Jessica had raised her hand in math class and told her mathematics teacher that she disagreed with something he had stated. She articulated her thinking with evidence and the teacher acknowledged his mistake. Since that time, I have visited with Jessica on several occasions and she invariably tells me she misses the stories, longs for our big "problems," and that without those pieces "math isn't as much fun." Jessica is one of many children who felt the impact of my newly implemented research-based instruction. The feedback and test results quantify that I am on the right path.

My heightened awareness of my own teaching techniques motivated me to start a monthly math meeting I call "Math and Muffins." Each month, in the hour before school begins, I meet with a group of interested colleagues to share ideas for successful mathematics instruction over breakfast. I always use a book with a strong female character, talk about how I incorporated the story in my math class, and present children's work. Math teachers are not my only customers, so the stories are being used in several content areas. As a result of these informal meetings, we have had more dialogue about what is happening with our mathematics teaching than ever before. The primary teachers are getting a vivid image of what students need to know to do well on the statewide tests when they enter fourth and fifth grade. In addition, teachers have stretched their thinking about what kindergarten and first graders are capable of doing mathematically. Most important, we are women supporting each other as we move in the direction of effective mathematics teaching that reaches more students, particularly females.

Our research has empowered me to take my ideas out of my classroom and disseminate them to a larger audience. I have helped coauthor articles and this book. I have spoken at mathematical conferences. All these events strengthen my resolve to keep the ideas coming and strive for lasting change.

Recently, our new principal read a story to my mathematics class. Occasionally, she would pause in her storytelling and ask the students to make predictions. When she finished reading, Joseph said, "Aren't you going to ask us about the math in the story?" This comment took her by surprise. She had never imagined that there was mathematics to be found in the treasured story she had been reading to children for years. She was also impressed with their in-depth thinking and their solid interpretation of the literature. Watching someone else read to my children also gave me a new lens with which I could examine my students. I noticed their ability to see patterns, think logically, and analyze ideas in print. They have developed almost as much as I have.

Linda has also experienced changes as the project progressed. Here are her thoughts:

Research requires personal reflection and evaluation. Throughout the last two years of this project, I have learned many lessons. I am constantly fine-tuning and refining my teacher talk and questioning skills. I have audiotaped many hours of my children in class and have found this a great way for me to reflect on my own teaching. An added benefit is that when the students knew I was taping they would also share more in-depth thoughts than on days I did not tape. I am far more critical about unsuccessful mathematics lessons and spend large blocks of time revisiting them to find out what was missing. But my story is more than this. Mine speaks of mothers and daughters.

"When are we going to have math, Ms. Allen? I want to work on the writing piece that explains how I solved my problem." Strange words to hear from a nine-year-old girl who came to my classroom two years ago and introduced herself by saying she hated math. Gretchen was a wonderfully gifted student in all the subject areas, yet she had already decided to hate math. She would wrinkle her nose and shake her head at the very mention of the subject. Unlike Gretchen, I have always had an interest in mathematics, but like Gretchen, I never developed confidence in my abilities to do mathematics. As a teacher, however, I knew that there were better ways to teach it, and I was determined to bring those strategies to bear on my work with Gretchen.

Through this project we grew more understanding of the ways girls learn best, and it made me realize that I needed to help Gretchen be more conscious of her own learning styles. I needed to find a hook. Using books about strong females was the answer. For Gretchen, children's literature became an indispensable part of her mathematics instruction. Together, we learned to find the mathematics in books and thereby learned to seek out mathematics in everyday situations. We now see math all around us.

In conferencing with the Gretchen's mother, I asked her if she saw any changes in her daughter's attitude toward mathematics. This mother had such positive comments in regard to her daughter's mathematics profile: "My daughter is eager to get involved with math now. She has a positive, I-can-do-it attitude. Math once was incomprehensible to her, whereas now she finds it stimulating and challenging." She went on to say that she felt this change was a result of the use of writing and thinking skills, being positive on the home front, and having good women role models. She emphasized that the more female role models there were, especially in the areas of math and science, the more acceptable it was for a young girl to excel in these fields. In addition, she expressed her feelings that we must start early to encourage girls, building their confidence early on. Gretchen's mother felt her daughter would definitely succeed due to her newfound confidence in her math abilities.

When this team of writers came together as teachers and learners we found we were seeking answers to a common question: How do we foster confidence, perseverance, and understanding in our female students in the area of mathematics? It was at that time I was already noticing a distinct lack of confidence affecting my own adolescent daughter. She did not want her mathematics teachers to discover that her mother taught mathematics too. Since my daughter was such a "good girl" in class, teachers frequently showed surprise when she expressed her intense dislike for math. I was certain that I needed to find a solution for my child while finding a solution for all of our feisty daughters.

At home, my daughter and I had many long conversations at the kitchen table, trying to reconstruct what she had tried to learn in math that day. She seemed to be disconnected from the instruction and did not have a desire to discuss her concerns with the teacher. I decided I could no longer sit by while her self-confidence in mathematics eroded. I wanted her to establish her own voice and take the risk to say, "Show me another way." I decided to read her the stories I was reading in class and gave her articles and books on females' learning styles that I was reading with my colleagues. As a result, she is now more aware of her own role in her progress and is no longer content to be a passive learner. She speaks up when she thinks the teacher is not clear and on her own initiative pushes to find other approaches to help visualize the concepts. My daughter's math grades and test results even surprise her at times.

The research, the study, the writing, and the sharing that went on as we worked toward this publication has afforded me opportunities for which I am very thankful. Speaking at regional and national mathematics conventions, authoring an article for a mathematics journal, conducting workshops in my own district and across the state, and working with parents and students (moms and daughters) in new and challenging ways has changed the way I think of myself.

The multiple benefits we have identified through our work have also been documented by others.

There is evidence that the expectations and actions of a single teacher can make a tremendous difference in the lives of students. Working to support the full development of girls and boys can empower not only students, but the adults who work with them. Undertaking the process of examining how gender bias affects students also involves looking at ourselves and the institutions in which we operate. The realization that we can make change within the classroom and the school often leads to a feeling of empowerment that extends beyond the school to the larger community. Many gender-equity advocates say that their work on this issue has enhanced their personal as well as professional lives. (Wheeler 1993, 13)

Thinking Like a Mathematician

Many adults and children view being a mathematician as having operational skills at their disposal. Mathematicians are those people who can find "answers" to problems quickly and efficiently, who recite the appropriate rule for the corresponding problem, and who can flip, slide, rotate, and tessellate at will. After working in mathematics classrooms where all children are seen and see themselves as mathematicians, this limited view of a mathematician becomes rather obsolete.

At first glance, Thylias Moss' book *I Want to Be* doesn't appear to be filled with mathematical ideas. There is, however, a strong similarity in how other people view a child's answer to "What do you want to be when you grow up?" and "What is a mathematician?" In response to the first question, the child in Moss' book does not answer in a typical fashion. She thinks not of making a career choice, but instead sees herself entering the adult world with characteristics that allow her to view her surroundings through the five senses and to joyfully learn everything about the environment around her. She is not only imaginative, but daring in her descriptions.

> I want to be old but not so old that Mars and Jupiter and redwoods seem young. I want to be fast but not so fast that lightning seems slow. I want to be wise but not so wise that I can't learn anything.

Just as the girl in *I Want to Be* sees herself as much more than a person in a definite career, our students see themselves as people more able to function as mathematicians than the adults around them believe.

Our students wanted this book read over and over. The pictures drew them in, the poetry was magical, and they worked hard to see if we had chosen a book with hidden mathematics wisdom. The conversation was lively and at times not overtly mathematical.

> MS. ALLEN: Does anyone see any connections to mathematics in Ms. Moss' book?
>
> NINA: She says she wants to be "as big as" but you can always be bigger or smaller than something else. I guess that's math.
>
> NATHANIEL: There's a train in the story so you could find out about how fast trains can go.

NATALIE: There are designs on the kite like in geometry.

MACKENZIE: She said she wanted to be weightless and that means zero, and zero is math.

MS. ALLEN: I would agree that those are all ideas for mathematics in this story. Let's think for a minute about your thoughts the first time the story was read. When the adults asked the little girl what she wanted to be, what do you think they expected to hear?

PATRICK: They thought she'd say a firefighter or a teacher or a nurse or something.

NELSON: That's not what she was thinking though. She was thinking about being bigger than or faster than or smarter than something.

We continued by directing the discussion toward how students see a mathematician. We pointed out that at the beginning of school some of the students had written what they thought a mathematician was. Several students got out their journals and looked for that early piece of writing. These students shared what they had written.

SARAH: A mathematician likes numbers, can tell time, add, subtract, multiply, divide, make equations, and solve problems.

SEAN: A mathematician can read really big numbers, do fractions, and decimals, and use a calculator.

MS. ALLEN: What if I said that the answers you had early in the year seem just like the answers that the adults were expecting from the little girl in the story? Instead, she surprises them by explaining those "inside characteristics" that she liked. What inside characteristics would a good mathematician have?

GRETCHEN: A mathematician never gives up.

COOPER: You have to think about your thinking.

ASHLEIGH: You have to talk and share and ask questions like we do in our groups.

NINA: You have to really believe in yourself.

The discussion continued as children really started seeing themselves as mathematicians who had qualities other than being able to do computational work. Their homework assignment was to share these thoughts with their parents and to return to school with some ideas of how they could prove that they have grown as mathematicians.

The following day the students were ready to share their parents' thinking and they were ready to begin communicating in writing how they had developed as mathematical thinkers. In Megan's writing she points out, "I really concentrate to make my math make sense." Kevin explains, "I have also built up some great skills like cooperation because I work in groups well and always listen to what everybody says." Desiree defines her learning style in language we have used about multiple intelligences: "I am linguistic and visual, meaning I need to read the problem, rather than having someone else read the problem to me." Lauren illustrates her growth by saying, "I used to not like math at all, and now it is becoming my best and favorite subject." Writing as a reflection on a year's worth of growth in mathematics is a tremendously effective way to share with parents and teachers what our children really know and really can do.

Conclusions

We are pleased that our project has helped us poke holes in some of the traditional myths about females' mathematics performance. In reality, girls can meet with mathematics success while building confidence. Many teachers recognize that they can become too protective in an effort to shield girls from failure. Although this is not prompted by bad intentions it is a problem for females. Clearly, it is the subtle rather than the overt behaviors that should be unmasked and counteracted.

We are also working on modeling feedback that keeps girls from being praise junkies, addicted to comments such as "I like your hair" or "I like your outfit." We suggest teachers and parents focus more positive feedback on academically related activities and good decision making in all aspects of girls' lives. Also, when possible, parents and other significant family members should be cautioned as to the potency of comments such as "I was never good at math." Innocent sharing of such sentiments becomes a real handicap in the classroom.

The media and society will continue to discourage females in mathematics-related activities; teachers and parents must end the silence. They must not fail to encourage girls to be risk takers, problem solvers, and logical thinkers. As adapted from *Growing Smart: What's Working for Girls in School* (1995) the American Association of University Women suggests that educators, parents, and communities work together to create programs that

- Celebrate girls' strong identity
- Respect girls as central players
- Connect girls to caring adults
- Ensure girls' participation and success
- Empower girls to realize their dreams

Gender equity is about "enriching classrooms, widening opportunities, and expanding choices for all students. The notion that helping girls means injuring boys amounts to a defense of a status quo that we all know is serving too few of our students well. Surely it is as important for boys to learn about the contributions of women to our nation as it is for girls to study this information" (Bailey 1996, 75–76).

Through the work shared in this book, we are seeking ways to eliminate the roadblocks and hurdles that limit the options for both sexes. Males can look at what other males or females are doing and feel fully able to attack similar situations. On the other hand, females often perceive only what they see other females doing as being a possibility for them. If teachers wish to develop the underlying traits that strengthen the problem-solving abilities of females, they need to look at ways to introduce female characters in literature and real people with hardy personalities into their instruction. Clearly, there is a necessity to include female role models in classrooms so that teachers meet the needs of all children. Repeatedly, as we seek ways to help create more equitable classrooms we find the means of helping all students become more mathematically literate.

The President's *Goals 2000 Report* (1994) calls for the United States to be first in the world in mathematics by the year 2000 and to promote a significant increase in females and minorities entering mathematics, science, and engineering careers. Indeed, if these goals are to be reached, there is a critical need to create learning situations that encourage all children to be a part of the equation. Perhaps through the establishment of links between "feisty females" and mathematics, an important piece of the puzzle can be identified.

Works Cited

AMERICAN ASSOCIATION OF UNIVERSITY WOMEN. 1995. *Growing Smart: What's Working for Girls in School*. Washington, DC: The American Association of University Women Educational Foundation.

BAILEY, SUSAN McGEE. 1996. "Shortchanging Girls and Boys." *Educational Leadership* 53 (8): 75–79.

DORNEY, JUDITH A. 1995. "Educating Toward Resistance: A Task for Women Teaching Girls." *Youth and Society* 27 (1): 55–72.

NATIONAL EDUCATIONAL GOALS PANEL. 1994. *The National Education Goals Report*. Washington, DC: National Education Goals.

WHEELER, KATHRYN A. 1993. *How Schools Can Stop Shortchanging Girls (and Boys): Gender Equity Strategies*. Wellesley, MA: Center for the Research on Women.

Children's Literature

MOSS, THYLIAS. 1993. *I Want to Be*. New York: Dial Books for Young Children.

Appendix

Spreading the Words

During the 1930s a packhorse library was established in Kentucky for people in remote areas. Women on horseback rode into the secluded hollers and isolated corners of the state carrying books in saddlebags. They brought literature to families across the Commonwealth who would not normally have access to reading materials. In the spirit of the Kentucky Bookwomen, we share with you some additional books about feisty females that we have enjoyed and some of the mathematical connections with which you might like to experiment.

Bunting, Eve. 1989. *The Wednesday Surprise*. New York: Clarion Books.

Story line: Anna works in collaboration with her grandmother to prepare a birthday surprise for her father. Every Wednesday night, Anna and her grandmother sit together on the couch and read a story out loud. The surprise is not Anna's surprise but her Grandmother's. When the birthday arrives, it is Grandmother who stands and reads for the very first time.

Mathematics: This book shows young and older readers the importance of initiative and effort. Collecting data from a community of readers could be a focal point of investigating the number of books read or even the genre of books read during a certain period of time. Students can try sampling activities using books to find out the number of words on a page, average number of pages in a book, or the most frequently used letter or vowel. Analyzing that data would be very interesting during National Book Week or in conjunction with other library activities.

Caines, Jeannette. 1982. *Just Us Women*. New York: Scholastic.

Story line: Aunt Martha and the narrator plan a car trip to North Carolina. They carefully map out their route, pack their food, and talk about all the things they will do along the way. They look forward to the freedom of picking mushrooms and walking in the rain.

Mathematics: Invite a guest speaker from an automobile club to talk about planning a trip. Students can plan a car journey and calculate mileage and figure cost of gas, food, and lodging. If the timing is right, students could make this plan for an actual trip their family is taking.

Chang, Ina. 1991. *A Separate Battle: Women and the Civil War.* New York: Scholastic.
Story line: This book is a collection of stories of women from the Civil War era. The use of diaries, letters, and photographs captures the lives of women who influenced the course of the war: Women who took risks to care for wounded soldiers in battle, smuggled supplies and information across enemy lines, arranged funding for disaster relief, and maintained businesses for men at war.
Mathematics: Compare the statistical data for loss of life in the Civil War to wars since that time. Students could make a time line of the key battles and chart the loss of life over the course of the war. Find out the average wages for a nurse or teacher in the Civil War era. What would that wage purchase in today's marketplace?

Coerr, Eleanor. 1977. *Sadako and the Thousand Paper Cranes.* New York: Dell Publishing Co.
Story line: This historical book tells about a survivor of Hiroshima. Sadako has a zest for life. She trains and dreams of joining the junior high school racing team. Her life quickly changes when she is diagnosed with leukemia. She courageously tries to fold one thousand paper cranes so that she will be granted her wish to become healthy again.
Mathematics: The concept of collecting one thousand of something can lead to many mathematical connections. Origami, the ancient art of paper folding, can explore symmetry, angles, and congruent figures.

Cooney, Barbara. 1982. *Miss Rumphius.* New York: Puffin Books.
Story line: Miss Rumphius was the great-aunt to the storyteller in this book. She promised as a young girl to do three things: travel to faraway places, live by the sea, and make the world more beautiful. She accomplishes all three wishes, including her promise to her grandfather, by planting lupine seeds wherever she travels.
Mathematics: Students can explore distances to faraway places, flight costs, and modes of transportation. Students can explore the cost of city beautification projects and environmental cleanups. They also can experiment with the germination rate of seeds.

Forest, Heather. 1990. *The Woman Who Flummoxed the Fairies.* San Diego, CA: Harcourt Brace and Company.
Story line: This hundred-year-old Scottish folktale introduces us to the magical world of the fairies. The King of the Fairies hears about the wonderful cakes of the bakerwoman. He sends his army out to capture the bakerwoman. She falls into the

fairies' world beneath the earth and the king demands that she bake a cake. She does not put up with such demands! The tale has a happy ending, and we see the baker-woman's wily nature emerge.

Mathematics: Students can explore the mathematics in baking cakes. Examine recipes and look for patterns in the ingredients. Students can compute quantities to increase or decrease recipes. The students can be introduced to and discuss different units of measurement for volume and weight.

Gray, Libba. 1995. *My Mama Had a Dancing Heart*. New York: Orchard Books.

Story line: The mama in this story shared her love of movement and nature with her daughter. The story follows mother and daughter through the seasons and shows the dances they created in the rain, sand, leaves, and snow. The strength of the mother-daughter relationship echoes in these pages.

Mathematics: Combining mathematics with movement can introduce students to many patterns. Students could chart square dancing movements by observing and participating. Students can attend a ballet or dance performance, or a choreographer can be invited to visit the class and talk about patterns in dance. Students could create their own pattern of movement through stomping feet, clapping hands, twirling arms, or spinning their bodies.

Hoffman, Mary. 1991. *Amazing Grace*. New York: Dial Books for Young Readers.

Story line: Grace faces a dilemma when she auditions for the class play. Her goal is to have the role of Peter Pan, but other classmates tell her that she cannot play the part. Grace shares her desire to be Peter Pan with her grandmother, who shows Grace that she can grow up to be anything she wants. Grace not only enters the try-outs, but she also earns the part.

Mathematics: Students could survey parents and friends and invite them to talk about how they use mathematics in their careers. They can also discuss the characteristics necessary to succeed in different fields. Students can find out what mathematics is required for various college majors and careers. They can compare the skills used by mathematicians such as being creative, logical, and cooperative to skills needed for other jobs.

Holleyman, Sonia. 1992. *Mona the Brilliant*. New York: Doubleday Books for Young Readers.

Story line: Mona is an industrious entrepreneur who starts a business to earn money for a new bicycle. Her outrageously styled hair does not help her "hair cutting" business. She tries various ways to attract customers. Her "can-do" attitude and multiple problem-solving approaches present a positive role model for young mathematicians.

Mathematics: Students can explore combinations by trying to find out how many haircuts, perms, and colors Mona would need to do to earn twenty dollars. Students could design their own brochure to advertise their own businesses.

Houston, Gloria. 1992. *My Great Aunt Arizona*. New York: HarperCollins.

Story line: Arizona was born in the Blue Ridge Mountains and loved to read, sing, and grow flowers. She dreamed about traveling to faraway places. She does travel to her Aunt Sara's to study to become a teacher, and returns to teach in the one-room schoolhouse she once attended. Arizona stays and teaches there for fifty-seven years. She shares her love of reading, numbers, and dreams of faraway places with her students. Although she never traveled to all the places she dreamed, she goes with her students through their imaginations.

Mathematics: Aunt Arizona touched many lives in her fifty-seven-year teaching career. Students could interview teachers and calculate the number of students' lives these teachers touched in their careers. The survey should include beginning teachers, experienced teachers, middle and high school teachers, and private school teachers. Students could select a faraway place they would like to visit and determine the distance and time it would take to get there.

Johnson, Anne. 1993. *Cat's Cradle*. Palo Alto, CA: Klutz Press.

Story line: The rich history of string games comes alive in this how-to-do book. This book is for all people who like to try their hand at some classic string designs.

Mathematics: Taking a bird's-eye view of the string designs and putting them down on paper can help young mathematicians identify patterns, tessellations, and geometric shapes. The open loops of string can be manipulated to make regular two-dimensional figures, such as triangles, squares, and trapezoids.

Kidd, Nina. 1991. *June Mountain Secret*. New York: HarperCollins.

Story line: Jen shares a day of fly fishing with her dad. She learns the special tricks for catching rainbow trout. This colorful book also uses scientific names of many water creatures as a way to teach the reader about the freshwater environment. At one point in the story Jen becomes impatient and wants to give up. However, her father works with her and together they catch a rainbow trout.

Mathematics: Students could research or interview someone from a fish hatchery to collect numbered data about fish: How fast do fish grow? How big do the fish have to be before being released? How quickly do they multiply? They may also find out about migratory fish, discovering the distances they travel each year, and the period of time it takes them to get to their destination. Students can investigate conservation laws in their state and find numbered data that is included in the statutes. Conservation officers can be invited to come and talk about the laws and what mathematical skills they use in their job.

Lyon, George Ella. 1994. *Mama Is a Miner*. New York: Orchard Books.

Story line: Mama has a nontraditional job as a coal miner. Through lyrical verse, her daughter tells how she wishes her mother still worked a safe job at the store. Mama explains it is "hard work for hard times." The mother shows her determination and strength in providing for her family.

Mathematics: This story follows a sequence of events in the mother's workday. Students could compare work schedules between members of their families, showing what is being done at certain times of the day. Students could also look at elapsed time, time zones, and even the meter of the lyrical verse used to tell the story. Since this book has many interesting facts about coal mining, the students might work with measurements of coal, depth of the mines, and wages paid to coal miners. Students can develop a survey to find out how people heat their homes.

McCully, Emily Arnold. 1996. *The Ballot Box Battle*. New York: Alfred A Knopf.

Story line: Cordelia lives in Tenafly, New Jersey, in 1880. She visits her neighbor, Elizabeth Cady Stanton, and receives a riding lesson on Stanton's old mare, Jule. Cordelia also learns about Ms. Stanton's childhood, and how hard she tried to show her father that girls were just as courageous and smart as boys. Cordelia visits Ms. Stanton on election day and follows her to the polls to watch as Ms. Stanton tries to vote. While there Cordelia hears the taunts of boys about "no votes for pea-brained females." In response, she mounts old Jule and to the amazement of the crowd, courageously jumps a four-foot fence.

Mathematics: The historical background of this story could lead to a time line to show how many elections were held where women could not vote compared to how many elections since they started voting. Students can contact the election bureaus of the county and state and request statistical data on the number of women and men voting. Research can be conducted to find the number of women elected officials in their city, county, and state. This data could then be compared to data from another state.

McCully, Emily Arnold. 1996. *The Bobbin Girl*. New York: Dial Books for Young Readers.

Story line: Rebecca is the feisty ten-year-old working in a hot and noisy cotton mill. She is determined to help her family out financially, but conditions at the factory are making workers ill. Management is considering lowering the workers' pay. Rebecca's courage and desire fortify her as she decides to work with a group of women to protest the pay cut.

Mathematics: The story integrates social studies and mathematics. Students can explore the wages given to workers during the 1830s and create a time line of pay increases to the present. Other questions that children might explore would be: What was the length of the workday in a factory during the 1830s? Was there a minimum wage set for the workers? How old did you have to be to work in a factory? Were there laws to protect factory workers?

McKissack, Patricia. 1988. *Mirandy and Brother Wind*. New York: Alfred A. Knopf.

Story line: Mirandy is going to dance her first cakewalk. She vows to have the wind as her partner. She tries to capture the wind with Ma Dear's quilt, bottle it in a cider jar, and trap it in the henhouse. Mirandy uses the wind to help win the cakewalk contest.

Mathematics: Students can explore wind speed and how to use and read an anemometer. Students can construct pinwheels to use as a nonstandard measure of wind speed. They can record the number of rotations of the pinwheel on various days. Students could research and find out about the cakewalk dance, answering such questions as: How did the dancers use the square? and What was the rhythm of the music?

McLerran, Alice. 1991. *Roxaboxen.* New York: Scholastic.
Story line: Marian had a wonderful imagination and her make-believe town of Roxaboxen became the neighborhood gathering place. Children created houses and streets from rocks and boxes. The children, led by Marian, have a micro-society with money (pebbles), wars, speed limits, and even a cemetery for one dead lizard.
Mathematics: Students could make a map of what they imagined Roxaboxen to look like and use a map key with a scale. Students could create their own community map and make a guide to the town using coordinates. Roxaboxen used pebbles for currency, students could develop a class currency and make or bring in products to advertise and sell. Students could research the history of currency.

Medearis, Angela. 1990. *Picking Peas for a Penny.* New York: Scholastic.
Story line: Angelina and her brother are earning a penny for each pound of peas they pick. With rhymes, they keep counting the peas, one through ten, and have races to collect the most, even in 100-degree temperatures. She dreams of earning "ten tens," which she knows makes a dollar. Angelina shows us the value of collaborating to accomplish hard work, and keeping a positive attitude.
Mathematics: The rhyming text and consistent counting to ten make this a good book for primary students. The concepts of place value are introduced with the idea that ten tens make one hundred. Students could work with seed piles and calculate addition and subtraction problems. Older students could explore the economics of what a penny could buy in 1930 as compared to today. Students could compare and contrast the number of items it would take to equal a pound.

Oram, Hiawyn. 1992. *Reckless Ruby.* New York: Crown Publishers.
Story line: Ruby's parents tell her she is so precious that they want to wrap her in cotton so she can marry a prince. Ruby would rather make her own decisions. She consults her friend Harvey and he advises Ruby to be reckless instead of precious. Ruby showcases her feistiness by dangling from skyscrapers by her shoelaces, eating porcupines, and climbing into a python's cage. Many stitches and broken bones later her parents announce that she is not so precious and will not marry a prince. Ruby proudly proclaims that she can stop being reckless and grow up to be a firefighter.
Mathematics: Students could investigate statistics about children and accidents on a statewide and schoolwide basis. Primary research could be conducted to determine the number of classmates who have had broken bones, stitches, and hospital stays. Children could also research bicycle safety, including the use of helmets in the

school population. Ratio and proportion can be the topic in a comparative investigation between the wheel of a skateboard and that of a bicycle, or wheel-to-gear ratio in bicycles.

Rappaport, Doreen. 1991. *Living Dangerously: American Women Who Risked Their Lives for Adventure*. New York: HarperCollins.

Story line: This collection of stories tells us about six American women who courageously broke records and set new limits for adventurers. They show how the desire to achieve and succeed overruled the naysayers. The accounts from their personal diaries and newspaper stories give us firsthand experiences with courage.

Mathematics: The story of Annie Taylor going over Niagara Falls in a barrel can lead students to talk about probability of survival for daring feats. The maneuvers that pilot Bessie Coleman flew included 180-degree turns and climbing 200 feet a minute. This could lead to some research about flying. Eugenie Clark and her deep sea adventures can lead students to investigate and map the ocean floor. They could also research the creatures that live in the different depths of the ocean.

Ringgold, Faith. 1993. *Dinner at Aunt Connie's House*. New York: Hyperion Books for Children.

Story line: Melody takes us to visit her Aunt Connie and Uncle Bates in their beach house on Long Island. Melody delights in showing guests the talking portraits of famous, female African Americans on the walls in the house. The story is a time line of history. Melody shares her pride in her heritage and her hopes of someday becoming President of the United States.

Mathematics: Students can design a time line of the females in their family. This could be extended to incorporate research on famous female mathematicians and scientists.

Rochelle, Belinda. 1994. *When Jo Louis Won the Title*. Boston: Houghton Mifflin.

Story line: Jo Louis is sensitive about her name. She dreads the first day of school and telling people her name. She shares her fear with her grandfather, John Henry, who tells her the story of how she received that special name.

Mathematics: Students could collect data about popular names. The New York City Department of Health publishes "What's in a name?," a list of the most popular children's names in order of preference. Students could survey people from various generations and look for patterns in the popularity of names.

Rylant, Cynthia. 1996. *The Old Woman Who Named Things*. San Diego, CA: Harcourt Brace and Company.

Story line: The Old Woman had outlived all of her friends and was not ready to lose anything else in her life. She gave names to everything in her house that would outlive her including Roxanne her bed, Franklin her house, and Bud the new ceramic pig. When a scruffy little puppy appears at her house, Old Woman tries to shoo him away, but he continues to return to her. She keeps him around for quite awhile without a name, until he teaches her how lucky she has been to have known so many great friends.

Mathematics: This is a good story to use to discuss various ways to represent or name numbers. Children can be asked to represent numbers with two, three, four, and five digits in different ways, such as using manipulatives, drawings, and words. A good way to assess their communication skills would be to have them write a clear explanation of how they chose to represent the numbers.

San Souci, Robert. 1992. *The Samurai's Daughter.* New York: Dial Books for Young Readers.

Story line: Tokoyo is the daughter of Japanese samurai. Her father schools her in discipline and endurance. When she is sent to learn to be more ladylike, she complains and wishes she could live as a boy. Instead she is encouraged to spend time with the *amas* (women divers). She learns to hold more air in her lungs, and harvest abalone, pearls, and shellfish. When her father is exiled to the Oke Islands she courageously follows him.

Mathematics: Students can investigate lung capacity. Have students record data on how long they can hold their breath. This can be compared to the records for the longest amount of time humans have gone without air.

Say, Allen. 1996. *Emma's Rug.* Boston: Houghton Mifflin.

Story line: Emma, a talented kindergartner, can draw and paint. She receives many prizes for her art and shares her secrets for her creations. When her friends ask her where she gets her ideas, she suggests she just copies the ideas she sees in a treasured rug that was given to her at birth. When the rug is washed, it becomes unraveled and faded. Emma, believing her ideas will never come again, gives up on art and throws her prizes and art supplies away. She eventually realizes that the ideas come from within her, not merely from the design of a rug.

Mathematics: Students can survey their parents, teachers, and friends in an effort to identify and analyze their learning preferences, which they select from Howard Gardner's list of eight multiple intelligences. With this data they can construct a rug glyph to show their findings. Students can compare and contrast the rugs of their classmates. The information about students' multiple intelligences could be used to make a class chart of peer supporters.

Schwartz, Amy. 1988. *Annabelle Swift, Kindergartner.* New York: Orchard Books.

Story line: Annabelle listens to her sister, Lucy, give her advice on how to act the first day of kindergarten. Annabelle follows her sister's suggestions and the children laugh and embarrass Annabelle. When they are reviewing colors, Annabelle calls out Raving Scarlet, instead of red. But her ability to count money earns her the privilege of handling the milk orders on the first day of school. Through this chance to take leadership her confidence is renewed.

Mathematics: Primary students could work with equal values of money using a variety of coins. Students could identify money by size and shape. Older students could explore the difference in value between a stack of dimes and a similar stack of quarters. What are the combinations of coins you could have that would equal $1.08? What profit is made by the school from the sale of milk? How many milk containers could you purchase in our cafeteria for $1.08? Survey the cafeteria manager and chart how the price of milk has changed over the years.

Stamm, Claus. 1995. *Three Strong Women*. New York: Trumpet Club.

Story line: A Japanese wrestler sees a young woman on a country road. He decides to tickle her. She laughs, but then traps his hand and easily drags him back to her home. Once they reach Maru-me's home the wrestler learns about strength from Maru-me, her mother, and grandmother. These extraordinarily strong women have compassion and teach the wrestler how to be the best in Japan. He wins the emperor's competition and gives all the prize money to Maru-me.

Mathematics: This tall tale exaggerates what people can lift. This could lead to a discussion and investigation of the energy used in lifting and the different amounts of force needed when using a pulley, ramp, and block and tackle. Students could use spring scales to measure energy in Newtons and graph their results. Students can research the weight classes of wrestlers, and invite a high school wrestler to class to demonstrate weight lifting.

Sweeney, Joan 1996. *Me on the Map*. New York: Crown Publishers.

Story line: This story tells of a child's perspective of geography. Starting with herself, she expands to her room, her house, her street, her city, and so on. She includes a map for each area and relates, "This is a map of my street. This is my house on the map of my street."

Mathematics: The story integrates geography and mathematics. Students could examine various types of maps and look at scale. Students could try estimating distances and then make comparisons to actual mileage. This book also connects with "The Great Mail Race." In this activity, students estimate the distance and find the actual mileage on a map between their hometown and another. Then they write an informative letter and address it to Any School, city, state, zip, and wait for responses. Students could also make scale models of their rooms.

Thomas, Iolette. 1991. *Mermaid Janine*. New York: Scholastic.

Story line: Janine wants to learn to swim. Her parents enroll her in a twelve-week swim class. She follows her baby-sitter's advice and eats lots of vegetables and jumps rope to strengthen her legs. On the final day she passes the swim test.

Mathematics: Compare the speeds of strokes such as butterfly, back stroke, breast stroke, and free style. Outside, mark off the size of an Olympic pool. Have the children run the laps of 100 meters. Compare their running times with the time of swimmers for the same distance. Look into information about the distance swimmer, Susie

Maroney, who swam from Cuba to Florida in 1997. The students could gather information about her total swimming distance and her time.

Wetterer, Margaret K. 1990. *Kate Shelley and the Midnight Express*. Minneapolis: Carolrhoda Books.

Story line: Kate Shelley was a fifteen-year-old girl who lived with her family near a railroad track by the Des Moines River in Iowa. During a storm that flooded Honey Creek, Kate heard a train break through the bridge and fall into the flooded creek. Knowing that another train was headed that way, Kate courageously chose to make her way through the storm to get to the train station so that the express train could be stopped. Not only was she able to stop the express, but she also worked with a rescue team to save two men from the wrecked train. Kate Shelley is still regarded as a hero in the state of Iowa.

Mathematics: This story of heroism in a young girl will spark many discussions both mathematically and historically. Students can investigate train schedules, the number of railroad systems and trains in 1870s as compared with today, and the cost of transportation by train for a trip from one destination to another.

Widman, Christine. 1992. *The Lemon Drop Jar*. New York: Macmillian Child Group.

Story line: In this book, a little girl builds a close friendship with her elderly aunt. The child grows into an adult and reflects with her own daughter on the memories of those wonderful country visits. Her aunt's lemon drop jar was one of her fondest memories.

Mathematics: This story sets up a framework to engage young students with the topic of number. Students can explore estimation strategies with a simple plastic jar filled to capacity with lemon drops. Older students might strategize about the volume and capacity of the containers. The plastic jar could go home with a student over the weekend and he/she can return it filled to the brim with some item from home. The rest of the class (including the teacher) is then involved with a new estimation event led by the child who brought in the refilled jar.

Williams, Vera. 1981. *Three Days on a River in a Red Canoe*. New York: Mulberry Books.

Story line: Aunt Rosie, Mom, Sam, and the narrator take a canoe trip. In a scrapbooklike format, the narrator shares all the adventures and mishaps that happen along the way. The story is filled with number facts, a diagram for knot tying, and recipes for dumplings and fruit stew.

Mathematics: Students could plan a camp-out and find out about the costs and prepare a budget for the expenses. Students could create a booklet of problems that could be solved by using their budget. They can also compare the costs of camping versus restaurant and hotel costs for a similar vacation. Other problem solving topics could include figuring out the speed of river currents, fish size, and questions involving directions and orienteering.

Yolen, Jane. 1988. *The Emperor and the Kite*. New York: Philomel Books.

Story line: Djeow Seow is the tiniest daughter of the emperor. She is ignored by her older siblings and finds solace in flying kites by herself. When her father is overthrown and imprisoned, all the bigger and stronger sons and daughters flee. Djeow Seow is so tiny she goes unnoticed. She uses her kite flying skills to free her father and save the people from the evil rulers.

Mathematics: Students can construct traditional kites of paper and wooden supports, and record the height reached and the length of time they flew. They can also construct tetrahedron kites. Then students could investigate the various styles of kites, and if geometric shape affects variables such as the flight path. Students could experiment adding different amounts of weight to kites and observe the flight time and path.